THE POSITIVE ATTITUDE
Success Living
In Self Love

Dedication

This book is dedicated to Love, and to those who believe in being themselves and who never give up in life. I am grateful for love and life, which never stops teaching me to be in my Truth.

THE POSITIVE ATTITUDE
Success Living In Self Love

A co-authored anthology by
KARAMJEET KAUR
Self Love Specialist

The Positive Attitude: *Success Living in Self Love*

Copyright © Karamjeet KAUR, 2024

ISBN: 979-8-3390351-3-8
Imprint: Independently published

All Rights Reserved. No part of this publication may be reproduced, stored in a retrieval system, or transmitted in any form or by any means, electrical, mechanical, photocopying, recording or otherwise, without the prior written consent of the compiler, author, and publisher. The compilation of stories in this anthology are copyrighted material and remain the intellectual property of the author/s.

Editor: Karen Tants
Cover design: Bishal BK
Authors:
- ♥ Karamjeet Kaur
- ♥ Dr. Avanish Shukla
- ♥ Kathryn Cartwright
- ♥ Isabella Rose
- ♥ Rachel Moir
- ♥ Serena Lange
- ♥ Karen Tants
- ♥ Geri Magee, Ph.D.

Published by Healing Pen
On behalf of Karamjeet Kaur
Global Homeopathy Centre Sdn BhD
www.selfloveacademy.com.my
www.lovelifehomeopathy.com.my
03-80111550/0126952307

Acknowledgments

This anthology would not be possible if it were not for the love, support and collaboration of the amazing team of authors who co-wrote The Positive Attitude: *Success Living in Self-Love*.

Kathryn, Isabella, Rachel, Serena, Karen, Dr. Geri, and Dr. Avanish I wholeheartedly thank you for joining with me on this journey.

On behalf of my team of co-authors, I thank you, the reader, for choosing this book. Each story is a unique, yet individual facet of the one diamond, bringing you a deeper understanding of the meaning of self-love, the importance of having a positive attitude in life, and the healing power of faith, hope, and trust in your power to create a more enriched and positive life, no matter what challenges we may face.

Live, laugh, love.

—Karamjeet

Contents

Dedication ii

Acknowledgments v

SECTION ONE: *Karamjeet Kaur*

Understanding the Meaning of Living Successfully 9

A Positive Attitude Creates Success 14

Self-Love is the Way to Success in Balanced Living 19

SECTION TWO: *Co-authors*

Embracing the Change: My Journey to Self-Love and Empowerment
Dr Avanish Shukla *23*

How I Peeled back the Layers to Reveal My Self
By Kathryn Cartwright *29*

Loving Self Equates to Positive Transformation to Heal with Self-Love
By Isabella Rose *37*

Transforming Limited Belief Systems: A Gateway to Self-Love, Confidence, and Success
By Isabella Rose *43*

Hope and a Miracle
By Rachel Moir *55*

Interview with a Pranic Healer
By Rachel Moir *59*

No Matter how in Control I thought I was, God was about to Show Me Different
  By Serena Lange *67*

The Purple Monster Under the Bed
  By Serena Lange *87*

In Search for Meaning: Listening to the Guidance from Inner Self
  By Karen Tants *99*

You Are Your Own Sunshine
  By Geri Magee, Ph.D. *107*

About Karamjeet Kaur 118

End Notes 120

SECTION ONE

By Karamjeet Kaur

Understanding the Meaning of Living Successfully

By Karamjeet Kaur

"I want the feeling of success in my life.
I must work toward making it possible."

The above statement has remained on my mind since my early teenage years, when stories of successful people inspired me. At the time, success meant achieving great wealth and position, but life has shown me otherwise. I know now that the true meaning of success is living in self-love.

If you know me, you may have read the story of my journey and the one-night voice that changed me. Yes, changed me to think differently. A different view of life, ideas, different personality and much more.

Twenty years of loving myself through good and bad, improving through alignment within, has taught me the true meaning of Success Living, from my own personal context.

Ty Bennett: speaker, author, entrepreneur, says:
"The true definition of success is to become the best version of yourself you can become. The emphasis is on becoming, not on obtaining. Each of us has unlimited potential and it is the pursuit of that potential that is true success."[i]

Accomplishment is the feeling of satisfaction and fulfillment that comes from achieving a goal. There will be those who have no interest or aim in life; others have such amazing aim that they will do anything to achieve the satisfaction of success.

There is a 'thin line between success and failure', and it will be up to individual freewill of interest to reach that point. In simple terms, you must see and accept everything you do and the intention is already your success story. Be unconditional about the acceptance of successes in your life. Freewill means that you are free to understand your own acceptance of success even if it results in failure. Success comes from being yourself and appreciating everything about yourself along the journey to creating success in life. Don't be afraid of failure; failure is considered your Best Teacher. And as you understand that failures are your teacher, you are on the way to being a successful person.

Let's ponder further on the depth of meaning of failure behind every success story. You may have read stories of great people who overcame many odds before they were successful, and the list is long. They all must go through failure to understand the true meaning of success. Everyone believes success is the end of the story for those who live happily ever after. Let me remind you that the journey of life is full of surprises and difficulties. What is important is how resilient we are while we ride the waves.

Appreciate that every mistake, failure, and downfall guide you to hone your skills and habits, forming the best version of a self who is ready to walk through any challenge as a Successor (self-succeeding). Success lives for a couple minutes, or hours, but there are numerous faces of reality to go through in sustaining the core living of life.

Be ready to always be the Successor of your own life regardless of darkness that may step in. You will create a greater success story for yourself moving onward. Failure encourages you to recreate yourself so that you can embed success within. No longer think of failure as a big stigma; a big fear that no one wants to hear or see or feel or be it. We push ourselves carefully toward the path of success to avoid failure by being wise in our journey. There is nothing wrong with that but we must accept failure as the path toward success.

It is common to ascribe the meaning of failure as lack of success:

For example, lack of success means people may think you are unsuccessful. The terms of success here are if people think you are successful in life, then failure is not your image portrait. Conversely, being 'poor', seemingly unwanted, normal living that is not viewed as successful is the image portrait that can be seen in the community.

I used to think that it was necessary for me to appear successful to be accepted for being who I am. Along the way to achieving my success, this way of thinking made me realize something was missing. That 'something' was self-love.

By loving myself, the feeling of contentment has been as much within as it has been from the good success moments I have attained, and while doing my practices of affirmation loving myself, I found that the feeling that comes from achieving success lasts only moments in my life, but the true success that carries eternally and daily for me is knowing that lives are being saved through my work; seeing someone smile through my deed, hearing the sound of laughter in a room through my jokes, feeling that people around me are also feeling happy has made me content, more so than any 'material success achievement'.

I 'became' to understand that real success comes from giving back to others through being positive, feeling loving thoughts, embracing laughter, experiencing empathy, expressing kindness, embodying compassion, and much more.

Feelings of contentment and satisfaction through your success are yours truly and only when you can connect with the deeper meaning of it. In the material world, surrounding ourselves with the luxury of the material represents to us power. Yet the minute the success of material luxury begins to fade, a feeling of discontent arises, showing a different personality - of dejection and defeat.

Introspectively speaking it is not our birthright to feel defeated but encouraged that life provides a wonderful opportunity to improve oneself in learning the meaning of living life successfully. Here is my truth to you, value every success that comes your way; whether it is big or small, it never matters; what matters is for you to connect to that feeling and build the

THE POSITIVE ATTITUDE: SUCCESS LIVING IN SELF LOVE

contentment and appreciate totally as you practice concurrently the feeling of success in all moments, learning to really make your failure your good friend so you will know that success is the next step away. Be excited that failure is guiding you to grow your own muscles of success. Additionally, the practice of loving yourself in that way will make you aware that failure will always pass. You were born the Successor of your own journey. You have never known failure. You know the gift that you are. Make your 'success wings' walk, as you own it.

A Positive Attitude Creates Success

Our attitude introduces us to others. It affects all our interactions, how we approach day-to-day situations, and represents our way of thinking; either positively or negatively.

Attitude reflects in the feelings we have and the thoughts we think, combined with action as we express it. Attitude is the structure of the belief system we have held since childhood. Its growth molded according to our experiences throughout life. Therefore, it is important to understand the types of attitudes we have and our responses within and outside our moments and situations.

Success is available through knowledge via education but impacted by oneself via attitude. The reason is that attitude results from lifelong awareness perceived in every moment according to each circumstance and mind belief system. As I explained in *Understanding the Meaning of Living Successfully*, success is about contentment.

There are multiple levels of education. And the level that drives each human being is the level according to the behavior and attitude each of us display.

Here my aim is to encourage positive learning of your rightful knowledge of the attitude required to bring you to the greatest level. The following are examples of the attitudes required for career development and improving relationships:

THE POSITIVE ATTITUDE: SUCCESS LIVING IN SELF LOVE

- ♥ Humility/Humbleness — Humility brings feelings of empathy within and is grounding. Humility reminds us that we all make mistakes, and it keeps us from thinking we are better than anyone else.

- ♥ Openminded — Being openminded creates the space within to be flexible to understanding matters rather than being close-minded or rigid.

- ♥ Excited (all moments) — We are gifted beings, as I stated in my book, *Life is a Gift: Loving You*. As we accept the gift of ourselves to everything in life, the exciting feelings will always be arriving in you to look for more excitement in life. It truly matters to keep your joy flowing as you move along with your decision toward your success process, creating more worth rather than worry or doubt about it.

- ♥ Gratitude — It is important to feel gratitude in all that we do. Success will be easier as we practice gratitude in our ways. The more gratitude we practice the more success easily flows toward us.

- ♥ Willingness — When we resist where it comes from fear of the unknown, or of being unsure, naturally the willingness attitude becomes difficult to activate. In wanting success in your goals, willingness and a "Can Do" attitude is very important. Always create ample space for being willing to investigate new situations; you never know, it might be the cream of success you want to experience.
- ♥ Acceptance — No matter what happens along the way as we work toward achieving goals, we must accept that it only

happens to mold and make us better than we are. Acceptance allows the process of letting go, forgiving, and doubting to ease off so we become open to the flow of ease to success.

- ♥ Respect — Before we respect others, we learn to respect ourselves in all senses. When we stand at the door of success, sometimes we get carried away… for example, thinking we are above, or better than others. Now, as one respects the self, one will be more understanding and respectful of anyone from all 'walks of life' without judgement because we have been there also.

- ♥ Committed — Committed within brings profound success and worthiness to a level that one becomes stronger. The strength that comes from development to committing to all ways, creates more ground foundation to sustain every success.

- ♥ Giving 100% — Give full 100% of self to make things possible for self. Never give half in anything committed for success. Giving half means the success to achieve becomes half too. 100% must be genuine and come from love, knowing that one is doing it for self, from which arises satisfaction no matter the result.

- ♥ Responsible — Once we want an experience, it is important to be aware of our responsibility every step we take. Being responsible creates further capability and understanding of self. This brings immense motivation to keep creating betterment of life.

THE POSITIVE ATTITUDE: SUCCESS LIVING IN SELF LOVE

- ♥ Willing to apologize — As mentioned above, the attitude of willingness comes from being able to give in, to allow the self to move forward, to ensure there is space for letting go, for being sorry, or apology. We all unconsciously make mistakes in life that bring disadvantages on the journey making success happen. In the interim, we must be ready to learn to say sorry so we don't take it with us on the coming journey. Every success teaches us to learn to feel good with others.

- ♥ Stay grounded — Grounded is stable, balanced, sensible, and able to build safe boundaries. Practicing sensibility within helps us to make better decisions or choices to bring balance and harmony into our lives. It is important to understand this so that we can create better sustainability in our lives while we enjoy our success stories.

- ♥ Enjoyment — There is a school of thought that having too much happiness brings sudden calamity that takes away our right of being happy always. This is an old taboo. We must break this taboo. We were born a gift; embodiment as a gift means our birthright is to be joyous in life. When we are passionate about something we like to do, or the work we perform, or the relationship we are in, or anything in which we are connected, we evoke our joy that makes us more vibrant. This vibrant energy we exercise while being happy to do whatever we are doing while not worrying about any outcome. We are happy to be or do as it is; that itself brings the best success story of satisfaction that we ever dreamt about. Be the joy that we are so we keep creating more joy within and around us. I know it can be tough to be joyful every moment, especially when facing uncertainty. However, it is important to note that we can switch the button at any time by changing our thoughts around it.

- ♥ Patience — Having the ability to be in the moment no matter how tough it gets; its amazing ability brings much wisdom. Patience brings much sweetness to the process of success. It also helps us to be careful in making decisions on the choices we make. As we practice patience, we also create our ability muscles to be stronger as we walk through life. We have a goal to attain, and patience is the highest requirement needed to reach it. Patience teaches us to learn to sustain the feeling of success in a more harmonized way.

- ♥ Breathe — The more we practice breathing and being in alignment on our daily path, the more we further understand oneself and own vision. Focusing on the breath places awareness on the present moment, not on the past or future. It recreates the bonding of inner self and realigns self with every action we do for the path of success.

Always assess within first. Attitude develops inside oneself in every moment... moment to moment. Attitude can change so long as oneself is willing to change and expand herself or himself. I repeat: "Always assess within first", so there is knowing of oneness of self being observed within. This is particularly important guidance for every want, project, vision goal as one wants to experience along the way. It is always necessary to assess within, check beliefs and ideas we have before we move toward what we desire. Smoothing the process of achieving success starts from within.

Self-Love is the Way to Success in Balanced Living

" Self-love is all about eradicating the judging that we grow up with. It becomes an exciting tool to remove the 'no use' thoughts and to build our self for living our life. Judging self and others is the main barrier within that separates us from knowing our true self truthfully. We have thoughts that on a constant basis give ideas and perception which does turn to judgement. These judgement thoughts can be damaging or uplifting, it all depends on your selflove in you and the environment. So, it is important to learn to fully understand self through self-love. As you love yourself unconditionally, there are only good thoughts to bring better perception and idea of your perceiving around you. This will help you to create a better life for you and your contribution to the environment.

Love is unconditional energy. We are natural born love beings. We do not need to work hard to get love but only to be aware that we are love. Aware to accept, appreciate, embrace and grateful of happiness being as love. This awareness will be starting on its own ability when the individual who practices belief understands that true love is, as they, are."

— Truly Love Within (*Excerpt from Chapter One*)

We have free will to create our journey in any way we wish. By living life successfully, we experience life as good, feel harmonious, embody love, joy, empathy and understanding, and be empowered to create positive change in our own life and all others.

I mentioned before we are gifted. Being a gifted human being means we are already successful living on planet earth.

Self-Love has been a subject of discussion since ancient times, the first documented being Greek philosopher and polymath, Aristotle, 384BC-322BC.[ii] Aristotle distinguished true self love as in service to others (altruism), rather than selfish love, only concerned with love of oneself.

Every famous and successful personality has one thing in common: *They are fearless to be themselves*. Being fearless is about walking the talk. The process of success takes momentum from within from melding to aligning while standing firm in their convictions, practising the core living attitude of being in balance as much as possible. Their "Fearless" is always on point while standing in their Power Self.

As we practise the truth of self-love, a feeling of joy arises from within. When we focus on experiencing this joy any moment we can, we keep up momentum toward creating the excitement of living life as much as possible, it's a given. Letting go of the resistance of being open to every new expansion makes one believe Life is Heaven Afterall. It is all about embracing the self through all moments in learning and developing inner levels in a positive way.

Let's keep creating more success stories by being all that we are in a positive and loving manner. So, we lead our life in healthy competition rather unhealthy. The harmonious living becomes true for everyone. One by one, we begin to believe each can receive success and value every tiny success as greatness of self. There is Nothing to be afraid of but only to be aware of Self. Two important questions to check in with Self in every moment in life:

- ♥ Am I on the right path for myself?
- ♥ Am I hurting myself or anyone else with this decision/choice I made?

To keep probing the self means checking within your awareness as You know you are the in-charge person for self-ability to your path of success. There is no one to blame or be angry with because You are the One creating your Life. This is where the above attitude becomes your reference point and reminder always.

Never allow defeat to define you, it's not possible and that's an eternal truth. Only allow your power, this makes you your believer. You are born as successor despite any challenges you may be born with or experienced while walking on earth. Enjoy every moment of living as successor in being who You are. You are love, it's your truth.

—Karamjeet Kaur

SECTION TWO:

Co-authors

Embracing the Change: My Journey to Self-Love and Empowerment

Dr Avanish Shukla

In the pursuit of living a fulfilling life, few journeys are as transformative as the one toward self-love. It's not just a personal endeavour; it's a path that can illuminate the way for others, creating ripples of positive change within relationships, friendships, and professional interactions.

My journey to self-love and positive attitude has been a deep, introspective voyage, marked by moments of struggle, revelation, and growth. I invite you to explore the story of how embracing self-love became the cornerstone of my existence and how it continues to shape my interactions with the world.

Many years ago, I found myself trapped in a cycle of self-doubt and negativity. My professional life was stagnating as a lecturer and my personal relationships were strained due to time constraints.

Despite outward appearances of success, I was disheartened and disconnected from my own sense of purpose. It was during this time that I faced a significant crossroad—a period marked by choosing or deciding one pathway for my life. It forced me to confront my own vulnerabilities and prompted a deep reflection on what truly mattered to me.

This is the story of an ordinary man who now believes in himself more than anything else in the world after realizing the importance of self-retrospect. The journey starts with more than one decade of hardship in my career as not only a doctor, lecturer and family man, but also a businessman, scattered into every corner, unfulfilled, finally resulting in negative impacts on outcomes.

It was not uncommon for me to start my day in a completely perplexed state of mind, and by the end of the day, feeling tired and incomplete. I was working a full-time job as a lecturer at a university, my clinic demands full-time but I gave part-time to it. I supply medicines in Malaysia as sole dealer for a German pharmaceutical company. My work does not stop there, as a married man, my time is also divided taking care of family. This was me—a Jack of all trades and master of none.

Friends, I reached the stage in my 'rat race' that I am only increasing my egotism nothing else; monitoring gains are not fruitful as I did not have the time to enjoy it. Life was completely imbalanced. One must choose carefully what one's inner satisfaction is and follow that voice to achieve meaningful fulfillment.

Finally, me and my wife decided to reform the route we had been journeying. As many of you know, my wife already practices self-love, and has been for more than twenty years. I was in ignorant, egoistic mode so never mindfully thought of it.

We did a calculation of each task I am performing and looked keenly at the returns from each. Not only that, but also incorporated the returns concerning feelings so that I could feel accomplishment on an emotional level.

We concluded that one task would be to make our clinic a full-time business and let go of all the others now. Friends, it was not an easy decision to make but we took the completely transformational route. In the beginning of the new journey, we had doubts and frustrations, and due to financial insecurity I went back to teach in one of the universities part-time. However, as clinic demand was increasing I was able to be full-time at the clinic.

Tools and self-love practices during tough times

In the wake of profound loss, I began a journey of self-discovery. I started with small, daily practices: journaling my thoughts, setting aside time for self-reflection, and seeking out experiences that nurtured my spirit. It was through these practices that I began to unravel layers of self-criticism and negative self-talk. I learned to replace self-judgment with self-compassion, treating myself with the same kindness and understanding that I would offer to a dear friend.

One of the most pivotal moments in this journey came when I decided to embrace a daily gratitude practice. This practice became a sanctuary where I could connect with my inner self, observe my thoughts without judgment, and cultivate a sense of inner peace. Positive affirmation helped me recognize the beauty of my own existence and the importance of nurturing a positive outlook. Once I saw positive impact on my journey, I started sharing to my clients and with help of my partner/wife we have built a successful journey.

Agent of change

Embracing self-love also meant stepping out of my comfort zone. I began to challenge myself by setting goals that once seemed unattainable. I enrolled in learning new skills and took on leadership roles. I started to see that growth often comes from facing fears and overcoming obstacles. Each step outside my comfort zone became a testament to my own resilience and potential.

In my professional life, this shift in attitude allowed me to take on new responsibilities with confidence. I found myself more open to collaboration and innovation, and my positive outlook became a source of inspiration for those around me. In personal relationships, I noticed a profound change as well. By embracing self-love, I became more empathetic and supportive, fostering deeper connections with friends and loved ones.

The benefits of cultivating a positive attitude and self-love are manifold. I discovered that approaching life with optimism not only enhances personal well-being but also positively impacts relationships. My newfound self-compassion allowed me to be a role model for others, demonstrating how embracing one's true self can lead to authentic connections and meaningful interactions.

Living with a positive attitude also opened doors to new opportunities. I became more receptive to change and growth, allowing me to explore paths that I had once deemed too challenging. This shift in perspective has been instrumental in achieving both personal and professional success.

THE POSITIVE ATTITUDE: SUCCESS LIVING IN SELF LOVE

What moves my soul is the desire to help others realize their own potential. My personal belief is that self-love is not just a personal journey but a universal one. By embracing our own worth, we empower ourselves to contribute positively to the lives of others. My experiences have shown me that when we take the time to heal and love ourselves, we become beacons of light, guiding others toward their own transformative journey.

My journey to self-love has been one of profound transformation marked by growth, resilience, and a deep sense of purpose. It has taught me that embracing oneself is the key to unlocking a fulfilling life and making a positive impact on others. As you embark on your own path to self-love, remember that each step, no matter how small, brings you closer to the life you envision. Embrace the journey with an open heart, and let your own light illuminate the way for others.

AUTHOR BIOGRAPHY—Dr. Avanish Shukla

Dr. Avanish Shukla is an eminent homeopathic consultant, trainer and avid researcher. A second-generation homeopath, Dr. Shukla is the director and senior consultant with Global Homeopathic Centre in Malaysia. Dr. Shukla has been associated with the University of Cyberjaya for many years as a lecturer to students of homeopathy. Currently, he is appointed as a trainer in the capacity of building a program for homeopathic doctors (Nov 21 – Feb 25).

Dr. Shukla is a registered homeopathic practitioner under Traditional and Complimentary Medicine Council, Ministry of Health, Malaysia; registered homeopathic medical practitioner (H 27375) under Central Council of Homeopathy in New Delhi,

India. Completed PhD (by research) at University of Cyberjaya (Safety and Efficacy of Homoeopathic Preparation of Gymnema Sylvestre Q, 30 & 200 on Streptozotocin Induced Diabetic Rats). He holds a Bachelor of Homeopathic Medicines & Surgery from Bharati Vidyapeeth Deemed University in Pune, India in 2003. He has a post-graduate diploma in Hospital Healthcare Management from Symbiosis Institute of Health Sciences in Pune, India in May 2005. He completed his MBA – International Business from University of Queensland, Australia in July 2008.

Dr. Shukla's biography was published in British Encyclopedia titled: Successful People in Malaysia, published by British Publishing House in 2021.

How I Peeled back the Layers to Reveal My Self

By Kathryn Cartwright

I ran…
My fully formed brain's first adult act of self-love.
Running. An act I would not at the time consider self-love.

Yet, self-love required me to run—which I felt at the time was the act of a coward. Not the supposedly strong, independent young woman I thought myself to be.

What was I running from?
A broken heart, family relationships that I needed to navigate a different way, a workspace where I felt daily that it was sucking parts of me away and from myself?

Or from the layers that were layered upon my Self. Layers that had been added over the years to the point where my Self was so deeply hidden, that the layers had obscured my Self—like the numerous layers that animators would put on light boards to make certain that each frame was the next step in the film. Instead, my layers became so thick, so hard to see through that my Self disappeared to a mere memory and the other layers created the *who* that I became. A 'Myself' I didn't recognize. A Myself I wanted to erase from where I was at that moment in time.

And so, I ran. I ran to a different place, and I ran until I hit a proverbial brick wall that allowed me to not only remove layers but also to shatter against it. The shattering might have been needed as I have a healthy dose of stubborn and the guidance that might have been a little lighter; I ran from that guidance too—muffled it, pushed it away, and ran. I thought I was escaping but instead I went from one box to another box that mirrored the same lessons, but blunter, like a sledgehammer.

Eventually I discovered the running gifted me other lessons, and those lessons—while adding layers—gifted me with the need to remove layers, or else my Self would continue to be a mere flicker of my being.

Allowing *being* created *doing* in a different focus and manner than before. Allowing being created doing to come into alignment with my care of self. The act of self-love that had nothing to do with the picture-friendly form of self-care: bubble baths and massages and all those things that are so simple to do and not shattering.

The secret part though was the fact that I spent years running mentally until the physical need for running became too much and I acted. I took a flying proverbial leap off the edge into an unknown space and landed into the proverbial frying pan that was needed to sear away the need to hide from my Self.

My mental escape was reading: different places, different people, different worlds, different... anything different.

Anything to escape the 'now', where my emotions overwhelmed me, and my coping skills consisted of becoming into someone for the sake of another or escaping into other worlds—becoming that strong main character that could overcome everything when I wasn't certain that I could overcome the next morning. A childhood lesson learned and embraced and held onto for far too long in so many ways.

Paradoxically, intuitively I knew that reading and writing allowed my being to create my doing. The reading became a reason for doing. The reading became a reason for being and has been a simple way to do self-care since I was a child, beginning aged two. Precious moments of reading to the aging cat that would patiently allow itself to be dragged out from under the bed to sit with me while I read. Precious moments in college where I couldn't cope and would bring as many books as I could carry (from the library two blocks away) and binge read an entire weekend, hiding in my dorm room and being as quiet as possible so I could recover and recharge for more interactions. Until the balance was again needed between the desiring of interactions with others and becoming too much again.

That is how my life continued until the day I decided to run. Not to disappear completely since that was also always on my mind, but to run to a different city and see what it was like to start again; job transfer in place, apartment found, and a new start. But what at the time I didn't understand, was that my new start had the same flaw-some me at the center. The same fears, the same habits, the same everything other than space from people who knew me deeply and would have happily kept me tucked safely away in the little box of their view of me.

For several months, I experienced the ability to be more me versus less me. Until I didn't again, and then a new lesson, and a new set of life experiences where the old layers became reinforced and I stopped the doing of my Self and did the doing of expectations. Broken me, taking broken me without healing the parts and not understanding the parts that needed healing.

Broken me, learning to take actions that I didn't believe I would take to become a better me again. Years of working towards a better me once I realized that all my hearings of "not enough" and "could do better" and all those other hateful phrases that I didn't want to teach my children, and yet in the broken me time did say those things. Until two of my children in an innocent conversation brought a flicker back to my Self and that flicker wanted to shine clearly again.

Flickering brought the need for finding a way to heal, which meant I needed to love my Self enough that I could step into the hurts, the hidden parts, and the past with strength and gentleness for myself and others.

The saying, "hurt people hurt people", became a morning thought and how to ensure the hurts stopped and healed. The saying that I can only heal myself because we have free will became an afternoon thought. The saying that love is key became the before bed thought.

The teachings that I knew from years of reading, the teachings that I knew instinctively, the teachings that I would learn and embrace as part of my healing process bring all parts of me together instead of into separate buckets so that love became the key focus for all my life, not simply work, not simply home, not simply internally, not simply externally but all those spaces together, working as a cohesive whole. Even though there was a hole that was deep, each moment that I created a new rung to climb out, I realized there was a little flicker of light that I could see and I wanted to embrace it. Allowing my being to create my doing for a future me that would be whole again.

Yet, my inner work brought heart aches as people came and went, and situations changed so significantly that my prior 'false layered self' no longer looked as recognizable to my current self. I had to shift to more *me* and learn to release and let go of what I previously thought and allow the feelings to be paired with my new thought as my guide.

For example, a "No" where I would have always said "Yes". A 'Too Much' and being vulnerable when needed and allowing strength of self-love to be the motivator for what I would do. The past guided me and taught me so I could make better choices in the now for the future of where I want my path to go.

I spent days wondering if I was still broken. I spent days knowing that the gluing I thought I had placed (on a part) needed to be removed, and I needed to add in additional parts of healing. I spent days in relief that I knew love was there, that inner peaceful calm floating as I needed and called upon when the overwhelm threatened to be too much.

For the key to my self-love became the knowledge that I felt deeply, and what may be a surface scratch to someone else, became a deeper wound in some place that I might not have known needed to have my focus.

Moment by moment, day by day, baby step by baby step, those wounds began to heal as I did things to heal them, as I allowed myself time to be. Time to be with my thoughts and allow the jumbles to flow through, allowing the emotions to be part of who I was instead of walled off deeply into the nether regions of myself. Gifting myself with the permission to be enough for me and recognizing that no matter how much I loved someone in any of love's various forms and types, that I needed to be my own love to heal, which was hard, and still is hard. And opening my love to others to embrace those that hurt, through friendship and through writing, and through simply knowing that my guiding key is doing from a place of love and apologizing to others and to myself for those times I am not in that place. For allowing the hot molten lava of emotions to bubble up and reach that inner calm ocean of peace creating the new land mass for new seeds to be planted and grow in love's energy within me and allow that to carry out of me into the world. Because being in a place of love can be hard when the world tells you all the other messages.

Being in the world can be hard because of all the hurt people but walling my Self off and keeping others at arms' length and further is not part of my purpose on this planet. Embracing love and sharing that love with others, is.

For love is the key to our human life. A beautiful allowing of being and creating the doing of the moments of our self-love and embracing of our Self.

AUTHOR BIOGRAPHY—Kathryn Cartwright

Kathryn is a developmental content editor and a four-time Amazon bestselling author in eight co-authored books. She firmly maintains that the original voice of the storyteller is one of the most important parts of publishing. She also believes that everyone is a storyteller. Whether fiction, non-fiction, or technical manuals, all writing tells a story with the right content.

Kathryn started exploring developmental editing early in life. Her belief was that it would have been better to turn all the bad witches into good by loving them. Kathryn continues to share the love through her focus on developmental editing which allows authors to create stories that resonate with the world.

With having children, and actively volunteering with Girl Scouts, Kathryn's passion of learning and interesting conversations over a cup of coffee with friends with wide ranging topics bring her happiness. When Kathryn is not editing, she is likely to have her nose in a book, a kitten on her lap, and a cup of coffee or tea in her hand, soaking up the warm sunshine on the couch and enjoying a few minutes of peace. Once a year, she takes an unplugged vacation to a cabin with a beautiful lake, surrounded by pine trees and blueberry bushes, where cell phone signals are almost non-existent for a "being break" from the rest of the world. You can find more about Kathryn at www.writeadream.life, and her editorial services at https://www.writeeditshare.com
https://www.amazon.com/stores/Kathryn-Cartwright/author/B081TMCZ67
Contact Details: kacartwright22@outlook.com

Loving Self Equates to Positive Transformation to Heal with Self-Love

By Isabella Rose

Amidst the bustling rhythm of modern life, individuals often find themselves lost in the pursuit of wealth, status, or beauty. These are just an example of the endless societal pressures in today's world designed for us to "fit in," to be like everyone else, sending subliminal messages that convey we are not good enough the way we are. Commercials and magazine ads tell us if we buy this antiaging product, we will stay young and desirable or if we buy this type of car or wear this brand of clothing, we will be well-liked. It is no wonder why we—as a collective—often feel "not good enough."

This constant chase to fit in may lead to a negative self-image and a disregard for our own personal needs.

The antidote? Self-love.

Self-love is a concept often misconstrued as narcissistic or selfish. However, the essence of self-love lies in recognizing and addressing our basic needs, fostering personal and spiritual growth, and improving mental health.

Scientifically speaking, the term self-love refers to "self-positivity bias." This term refers to the tendency of individuals to associate positive information such as events, characteristics, and successes with themselves.

Jeffrey Borenstein,[iii] President of the Brain & Behavior Research Foundation—the largest private funder of mental health research grants—perfectly defines self-love as *"a state of appreciation for oneself that grows from actions that support our physical, psychological, and spiritual growth. Self-love means having a high regard for your own well-being and happiness. Self-love means taking care of your own needs and not sacrificing your well-being to please others. Self-love means not settling for less than you deserve."* (Borenstein, 2020)

Nurturing a positive self-perception or embracing self-love has endless benefits. Advantages of practicing self-love include:

- ♥ Enhanced mental health
- ♥ Greater self-acceptance
- ♥ Increased self-esteem
- ♥ Elevated motivation levels
- ♥ Stronger determination

THE POSITIVE ATTITUDE: SUCCESS LIVING IN SELF LOVE

- ♥ Heightened self-awareness
- ♥ Reduced anxiety levels

As I have learned through my own experiences in finding self-love and working with others in my workshops and coaching programs, despite the initial challenges and setbacks, anyone can learn to practice self-love and reap these benefits.

At its core, self-love is about managing our inner critic and inner judgement, developing a more forgiving view of our perceived failures, and appreciating our efforts and personal growth.

Here are five steps to help you foster self-love:

1. **Be aware of negative self-talk**: Notice when you are being too hard on yourself and replace those thoughts with kinder ones. Awareness is the first step in creating change.
2. **Create personal rituals/routines:** Develop meaningful and intentional practices, such as exercising for your body, meditating for your mind, or praying for your spirit.
3. **Establish healthy boundaries:** when those around you disregard your time or worth, it becomes challenging to practice self-love. Developing the ability to confidently decline requests and safeguard your time is an effective practice for nurturing self-love.
4. **Be gentle with yourself:** practicing self-compassion involves recognizing your struggles and offering kindness and understanding to yourself. It promotes personal growth driven by self-care rather than succumbing to feelings of worthlessness or unacceptance. This is an aspect I still find challenging at times,

particularly when I perceive that the long-term effects of a car accident are hindering my desired activities.

5. **Dedicate time for introspection:** when circumstances deviate from your plans, refrain from blaming yourself; instead, treat it as an opportunity for learning. Self-reflection can manifest in activities such as journaling, contemplation and meditation, regular reviews, or conversations with a trusted friend.

Self-love can significantly contribute to building happiness and self-esteem. Not only is self-esteem beneficial for children, but self-esteem is also equally crucial for adults. It enables you to set and achieve goals and maintain resilience in the face of setbacks. It reflects self-worth, your faith in yourself and your abilities, and your ability to accept responsibility for your actions. Adults with healthy self-esteem are motivated, set challenging goals, take pride in their accomplishments, and display tolerance and respect for others.

Having healthy self-esteem does not equate to being flawless or perfect; as human beings, we are perfectly imperfect so accept yourself exactly as you are. Find in the following list helpful strategies that I have learned in my journey to finding self-love that can help you strengthen your self-love as well:

♥ **Focus on your strengths:** recognize your strengths and positive qualities. Avoid comparing yourself with others the best you can and make a list of your accomplishments.

♥ **Take inventory**: identify and challenge any negative thoughts or feelings about yourself. Replace them with positive reactions and eliminate self-deprecating language.

- **Do something that makes you feel good every day:** engage in activities that bring you joy and interest you such as music, cooking, art, exercise, spending time with loved ones, or out in nature.

The following strategies can enhance happiness levels, acting as an antidote to stress:

- **Identify your unique "flow states":** flow is a state where you feel most creative and lose all sense of time. Identifying your flow state can help you recharge effectively.
- **Practice Gratitude journaling**: reflecting on things you are grateful for can foster optimism and happiness. Keep a journal to write down things you are thankful for daily. Make sure to include micro moments throughout your day such as a bird singing outside your window, the way the sun was shining through your window, the sound of your cat purring, your child's drawing they made just for you, or the moon and stars in the sky. I like to write in my gratitude journal at night before bedtime because it helps me relax, and my mind and heart are happy remembering the blessings the day brought. It also helps to set me up to feel good in the morning when I wake up.
- **Enjoy life's moments:** Take time to relish and fully experience the pleasures around you by simply being in the moment.
- **Strengthen resilience with self-care:** Resilience—the ability to adapt to challenges—is crucial for well-being. Prioritize self-care, including adequate nightly rest to enhance resilience.
- **Change your perspective on problems:** Instead of viewing difficulties as impossible hurdles, see them as temporary setbacks offering opportunities for learning and growth.

♥ **Learn from those you admire:** Seek inspiration from people you look up to, incorporating their positive qualities and strategies into your own life. Understand your purpose and support others.

♥ **Simplify your life:** Streamline your routines and leave time for uncomplicated joys. Keep your work and living spaces clutter-free for a more straightforward and fulfilling lifestyle.

Self-love can lead to better mental health, increased self-esteem, and improved life satisfaction. By learning to appreciate your hard work without being overly critical, setting healthy boundaries, and adopting self-care rituals, you can nurture self-love and reap the life-changing benefits. Remember, failure is not the end of the world; it is a stepping-stone toward learning, opportunities, and personal growth.

Transforming Limited Belief Systems: A Gateway to Self-Love, Confidence, and Success

By Isabella Rose

From the very core of our existence, our beliefs are shaped.

Beliefs form the lens through which we perceive the world, ourselves, and our potential. In this piece, we will embark upon a profound, transformational journey as we explore how changing negative belief systems into positive ones can be a catalyst for a life filled with self-love, self-confidence, and unbridled success.

Recently, while piecing together the rough draft for my second solo book, I was amazed to discover my belief systems had changed drastically over the past five years since the COVID-19 pandemic outbreak.

The stress of being "safely" at home deeply affected me. Prior to the pandemic, I was optimistic, happy, and always on the go whether traveling along the East Coast to facilitate workshops, volunteering in the community, checking things off my bucket list, or achieving another goal or dream.

Shortly after the quarantine was in place, here in the United States, I took an Immune Protection, Spring Health, and Detox class taught by Elson Haas, MD, and Sondra Barret, PhD. After class, I ran upstairs bubbling with excitement. I could not wait to share what I had learned about cells, viruses, the immune system, and more. The wind instantly knocked out of my sails when I heard, "Can't you see we are watching TV? We don't want to hear about it." My parents didn't share the same enthusiasm and excitement that I did and were not interested in me or what I had to share. What they were watching on TV was more important.

"I don't want to hear it" was a typical response I heard throughout my childhood and teenage years. But this time, their response shook me to the core. Instantaneously upon hearing this, the reality of experiencing quarantine hit me like a ton of bricks. It had been countless years since I had last received this type of response. It was a shock to my system to not only be around people who had no interest in me (and what I was doing or wanting to engage in meaningful conversations), but more so to be constantly amidst negative energy.

As the days passed in quarantine, I wondered how my mom did it 24/7 listening to my dad yelling and swearing all the time.

THE POSITIVE ATTITUDE: SUCCESS LIVING IN SELF LOVE

I could hear him, day in, day out, through the floorboards over my head and it began to weigh heavily on me.

(BS)abv: Belief System Formation

Bruce Lipton teaches and writes about the effects our living environment has on us in addition to our belief system (BS), cells, and epigenetics. Piecing together my memoir and reflecting over the past few years, I could 100% see it in myself. The false belief systems and conditioning of my childhood that I had worked so hard to overcome had begun to hard-wire themselves back into my brain, only stronger and louder this time.

Our beliefs form the foundation upon which our life is based. By the age of seven, most patterns of behavior and beliefs are already set. Our beliefs are not mere thoughts; they are the undercurrents of our actions, decisions, and emotions. Toltec tradition refers to them as 'our unconscious agreements.' Negative belief systems function as invisible shackles, holding you back from reaching your full potential.

The intriguing aspect of belief systems is their ability to become self-fulfilling prophecies. If you believe you cannot achieve something, your mind will find ways to validate that belief, leading to a life less lived. However, when you change your beliefs, you unleash the potential for transformation.

Negative self-beliefs function as unkind critics, consistently eroding confidence and self-esteem. They fuel self-doubt and insecurity, leading to potential impacts on physical and mental well-being. Taking the initiative to acknowledge and confront these beliefs marks the initial stride towards embracing self-love.

I have a highly active inner critic, judge, and perfectionist that has grown louder and louder over the past three years. I also have a "mean girl" whom I recently met through somatic healing with my therapist and art journaling. Interestingly, my "mean girl" is about seven or eight years old and has taken on characteristics and cruel things my father used to say to me during my childhood. She is extremely critical, and just not nice. She is hard to please, just like it was hard to please my father and mother and still is. Growing up it felt like I could never do anything right. My father led me to believe that I would never amount to anything and lacked talent, along with other false and negative BS.

Despite all this, I managed to accomplish my goals after graduating high school, including college. It was after leaving college that my life detoured. Finally, it took leaving a very toxic and abusive relationship for my life to really change for the better. I set my intention to learn how to love myself and take my power back from those I had allowed to abuse me (consciously or subconsciously). And that was what began to happen.

My heart and soul leapt with joy when I saw a Facebook ad in 2015 to become a contributing author in the 365 Moments of Grace book. But self-doubt kicked in with the conditioning rushing to the forefront... Who will want to read what I write? I'm not good enough or talented enough... etc. Even though I had one of my poems published in a book in sixth grade I was afraid to reach out and ask for more information about becoming a contributing author. Somehow, I found the courage deep inside and followed my heart and Divine guidance to reach out to the creators of the 365 Book series. And to my surprise and delight, they responded back! They were interested in my story ideas and would love to have me be part of the book.

Oh my God! Now what am I going to do? They accepted me! I thought to myself, why would they write back(?) never mind be interested in what I wanted to write.

My self-sabotaging mechanisms started to kick in and the false belief systems of my childhood had no problem stepping in to help. Who do you think you are becoming a published author? You're no one special. Dad is right I am not good enough or talented enough. Nobody will want to read my writing. Better to back out now when I have the chance. My mother's words echoed in the back of my mind, "How am I going to pay for this?" "Can you afford it?"

But I did not listen. I did not back out, instead I did it! I overcame the negative thinking and conditioning of my childhood! I followed my heart and Divine guidance to follow my dreams. I had written and submitted three pieces in that book. Little did I know that this would be the beginning of my writing career and making more dreams come true. Since the publication of the 365 Moments of Grace book, I have gone on to co-author eight other books, this will be my ninth co-authored book. I have also published my first solo book, Behind the Masked Smile: A Survivor's Quest for Love; a poetic memoir. I'm currently writing my second solo book. In hindsight, I can see that the 365 Moments of Grace book was my very own "saving grace".

Close to a year after leaving a toxic relationship and just over a year from making my childhood dream of becoming a published author come true, I was in what doctors say should have been a fatal car accident. Saved by Divine intervention and the power of love.

Tragedy struck again two months later when my fiancé was preyed upon by his so-called friends. He had texted me on Saturday night to say he was on his way home from Maine and would text me again later. Only he never did. Two days later, on his birthday, my world came crashing down around me. Matt died. I received the news from one of the people who contributed to his death. Matt relapsed and died of an overdose. In an instant, the future we had planned together was gone. The dreams we shared individually and those we held together. My best friend. My hero. The love of my life... gone.

As the days and months passed, I had opportunities to take the easy road and go back to the life I knew before Matt. But I chose to stay on the course. To stay committed to myself and the healing of my body, mind, and spirit. To continue to learn to love myself and to continue to take back my power. If you are unfamiliar with my story, Matt's love helped to transform my life and my belief systems, breaking generational cycles of abuse.

I had two amazing people in my life who continued to play an instrumental role in my healing journey: my mentors and editors of the 365 Book Series. They were the only two people I could trust after I left the abusive and toxic relationship before I met Matt. They were more than editors and my mentors. They were also my role models and cheerleaders. They believed in me when I could not even believe in myself, and as I continued to collaborate with them, I began to believe in myself again and gained self-confidence.

As a result of replacing self-criticism with self-compassion, I realised self-compassion is a cornerstone of self-love. However, over the three years of being with my parents during the COVID-19 pandemic, I began to hardwire the old conditioning of my childhood. All the self-confidence I had gained, lost; again, exposed to the same environment and people who created those false belief systems of my childhood.

The long-term effects of the car accident injuries began to overtake my life and get drastically worse. I was no longer able to perform certain tasks that I used to be able to do without limitations. And I certainly was not living up to my mother's high demands and expectations because of it. She had no understanding because I appeared fine from the outside. She understood when my arm was in a hanging sling after the car accident, but was unable to see the internal scar tissue, the limited range of motion in my neck and shoulder, or the cervical spine instability.

However, I learned to acknowledge my imperfections, treat myself with kindness, and accept my worthiness regardless of past mistakes and limitations of the car accident injuries. I paved the way for a loving relationship with myself once again.

Confidence is not innate; it is a belief in your abilities. The negative belief systems that eroded my confidence for years began to change after leaving that toxic and abusive relationship. As I prioritized healing the trauma and abuse of my past I began to transform my belief systems into more positive ones. I started to believe in myself and my abilities. The two writing mentors I mentioned earlier in this chapter played an instrumental role in helping me to do so. I was able to build upon that confidence even more by being in a healthy, positive, and nurturing partnership. By challenging my self-limiting beliefs, I began to unlock a wellspring of confidence I never knew existed.

Cultivating a growth mindset, with challenges viewed as opportunities for growth rather than threats, is pivotal for confidence. Something I learned not only from achieving my goals and childhood dreams, but also from the challenges I faced from the lifelong injuries from the car accident. Positive belief systems reinforce the notion that you can learn, adapt, and succeed, even in the face of adversity.

Negative beliefs often create artificial boundaries that hinder your progress. When you identify and dismantle these limits, you open doors to success you never thought possible like I did with becoming a best-selling author and having a successful opening reception at my first art exhibition. Changing my mindset in addition to inner healing work also helped me establish a healthy relationship and find true love with the man who was to become my husband before he died.

Positive belief systems align your vision with your goals. They help you see opportunities, seize them, and persist through setbacks. Believing in your capacity for success is half the battle won.

I hope by my sharing, I have illustrated through my words the profound impact that changing negative belief systems into positive ones can have on your life. It is a journey of self-discovery, self-love, confidence, and ultimate success. By recognizing the power of your beliefs, embracing self-love, building unshakable confidence, and setting a course for success,

THE POSITIVE ATTITUDE: SUCCESS LIVING IN SELF LOVE

you can transform your life into one brimming with fulfillment and personal achievement.

Remember, the beliefs you hold about yourself and your potential are not set in stone. They can be re-shaped, refined, and redefined repeatedly as I have learned through my experiences. You have the power within you to write your story, one positive belief at a time, and create a life that radiates with self-love, unwavering confidence, and the sweet taste of success.

You've got this!

AUTHOR BIOGRAPHY—Isabella Rose

Isabella embodies a deep passion for the healing arts and finds them wonderfully rewarding. Her passion flows as she touches people's lives and the world around her through her creativity, writing, and healing practices. She encourages and inspires others' creativity by touching upon the emotions, desires, and dreams held deep within their heart. In turn, they can move towards healing and achieving their full potential. She surrounds herself and others with positive energy. She builds community by bringing like-minded people together in her interactive workshops where she is "hands on," ensuring everyone feels safe, comfortable, and included.

Isabella has a diverse and extensive background in various alternative healing modalities including Angel Energy Healing, Reiki, Aromatherapy, and <u>Brain Tap Technology.</u> She holds a Bachelor's in Holistic Health Sciences and is currently enrolled in the Master of Natural Medicine Program and Doctorate/Ph.D. program at Quantum University. She has also studied with Dr. Elson Haas. She has undergone and completed the Recovery Coach Training through the Police Assisted Addiction and Recovery Initiative (PAARI) program and has Domestic Violence Advocacy Training as well as Trauma Informed Counseling.

Isabella's additional certifications:
- Warrior Goddess Training Facilitator
- Warrior Heart Facilitator
- Angel Oracle reader
- Angel Messenger
- Natural Rhythms Elemental Forces of Creation Oracle Reader
- Cosmic Smash Book Guide
- Therapeutic Art Life Coach
- Goal Success Life Coach
- Happiness Life Coach
- Life Purpose Coach

As a holistic health practitioner, Isabella specializes in empowerment and recovery, combining a variety of healing and creative art modalities for a unique experience tailored to the individual needs of her clients and students.

Isabella is the inspirational writer and best-selling author of the poetic memoir, **Behind the Masked Smile: A Survivor's Quest for Love.** She is also a co-author in nine books including the best-selling contributing author to the 365 Book series. Isabella featured in the best-selling book, **Soul-Hearted Living: A Year of Sacred Reflections & Affirmations for Women** by Dr. Debra Reble. She has been a guest contributor to DandiSoul and has appeared on the Global Transformation Summit as an expert speaker on Angels and Angel Energy Healing. She has also appeared on Enlightened World Network (EWN), <u>Cultivating a New Generation</u> podcast, <u>Re-Thinking Business: Success Sauce & Two Pickles</u>, and has been a co-host on the Angel Realms Radio Show with Maria G. Maas. She is a member of the International Association of Angel Practitioners.

Isabella resides in New England in a small town near Plymouth, Massachusetts where she finds inspiration for her writing and creative arts. She enjoys traveling, spending time in nature, and with loved ones. She loves cooking and baking for her family and loves to spoil her father's cat. She is an advocate for those who feel they have no voice. She loves helping others and volunteering for causes and nonprofit organizations close to her heart. Visit www. bellarosehealinghands.com to discover more inspiration and supportive resources.
Connect with Isabella on Facebook:
Bella Rose Healing Hands
https://www.facebook.com/Bellarosehealinghands/
Isabella Rose, Author, Artist, Healer
https://www.facebook.com/discoverthemagickwithin
To contact Isabella, you can email her at
bella@bellarosehealinghands.com
Author photo by Cynthia Wyman

Hope and a Miracle

By Rachel Moir

I only realised after having my fourth baby at nearly 40, how blissfully innocent I was at 27, giving birth to my first.
I never understood at the time why my partner was getting so many texts and calls to make sure myself and my daughter were okay. Why wouldn't we be okay? What could go wrong? Women give birth every day.

Well, I wish those thoughts had stayed true from the day she was born. Everything was good at first. Yes, birth was difficult, she was 'Sunny Side Up' so, they had a hard time getting her out. A failed vacuum delivery with a suction cup that flew off her head and hit the wall in front of us, followed by the pulling and dragging of a forceps delivery. She ended up in the Special Care Baby Unit for a few days, but nobody seemed too concerned.

When we got home, I did what I was told to do: "Breastfeed, breastfeed, breastfeed", from the midwives and "no she's jaundiced so she needs formula", from the doctors. So, wanting to please everyone, I did both.

After two weeks I was exhausted. I was so cold. I had blood in my breast milk. I was in a lot of pain and I went back into the hospital. They told me there was no need to take the antibiotics the GP has prescribed me, but just to keep breastfeeding to clear a mild case of mastitis.

Another week or so later and I could barely stand to change her. The coldness and pain were getting worse so I went back to my GP who told me to go straight to A and E. I left my newborn baby behind and waited in 'A and E' for hours. I was then referred to a hospital in a different city that had a specialist breast clinic. After being admitted and after numerous scans and blood tests, I was finally told I had a tumour the size of a melon in my right breast. I will never forget the look on the consultant's and nurse's face as they confirmed with each other what they were looking at.

It was so large they said, I would lose the breast completely as the only treatment for this type of tumour was complete removal. They weren't sure what my outcome would be. Then they let me go home. Still cold, still weak. I was to wait a week for a biopsy.

While I was waiting for the biopsy, I thought back to my teenage years when I ended up in hospital with septicaemia, from a nipple piercing that had gone terribly wrong. It felt very similar - the coldness, the pain, and the hallucinations. Luckily then, I had made friends with a very sick elderly lady who was in the hospital bed beside me. The day before I was due to go to theatre to get a large breast abscess removed, she had a visit from a tall man with a glove. He was with her for a few minutes and before he left, she said "Can you bless my friend over there too?". I had no idea what happening and just accepted the gesture, happy to be referred to as a friend from a lady I had only just met.

The following day the doctors decided I didn't need the operation. The infection had cleared and the abscess had almost disappeared. I asked my friend about the tall gentleman who had come to visit the evening before and she told me that we had both been blessed with one of Padre Pio's gloves. I found out that Padre Pio[iv] was a priest who was canonised in 2002 due to his ability to heal the sick. His hands and feet were marked with the stigmata and he had to wear gloves to protect the wounds.

So, with the little energy I had; after being told I had this tumour, my only plan was to get hold one of Padre Pio's gloves. I wasn't a bit religious, but this event had stuck in my mind.

I eventually managed to get a Padre Pio relic from a nearby church. It wasn't a glove but as far as I can remember it was something that he had owned or had a lot of contact with. I kept it with me until the day of the biopsy and prayed continuously to Padre Pio to help me.

On the day of the biopsy, they made about five piercings in what I called my 'third breast' due to the shape and size the tumour was taking. The following morning, I went in the shower and a yellow substance started spraying out from all the biopsy piercings. I ended up back in A and E and was put on intravenous antibiotics as I awaited the results of the biopsy. It was terrifying, but I still had faith that Padre Pio would help me out.

I was due to meet the consultant to discuss the results of the biopsy, but that was going to be another wait as the consultant was on annual leave and they didn't have anyone else there with the expertise. Given that I was so sick, the hospital arranged for a retired breast surgeon to come in to see me.

One of the breast care nurses knew how anxious I was and when I asked her for probably the tenth time if the results were back, she told me that she isn't allowed to give me the results, but not to worry as it may be good news. She then said I would have to speak with the breast surgeon to explain the results to me. I was slightly relieved, but still very confused as to what was going on.

When I finally met with the breast surgeon after another scan, he confirmed that it was good news! I was also met with apologies. Apologies and confusion from those who had 'misdiagnosed' an abscess the size of a melon as a large tumour. When they conducted the biopsy, they had burst the abscess!

I ended up with septicaemia again, due to the infection being left untreated for so long, but I was so relieved it wasn't a tumour.

I still to this day believe this was a miracle. A team of specialist staff, all agreed on the prognosis, so it wasn't just a single mistake from one. It was also a miracle I survived with no initial antibiotic treatment, as the infection which was an MRSA infection had spread to my entire body. I was still very sick and it probably took over a year to recover but I am so grateful to be able to tell this story. I'm still not religious, but Padre Pio has a very, very special place in my heart.

Interview with a Pranic Healer
By Rachel Moir

My friend has been practicing Pranic[v] Healing for years and I am fascinated by its effect on healing both individuals and en masse. It always seemed slightly covert, so I was excited to talk to Jennie about Pranic Healing and find out what it is all about.

Jennie Hannigan is mum to three fantastic boys and was also a foster mum for nine years. She lives in a picturesque cottage in rural Ireland with her children, and her dog, Roara, and cat, Shadow.

Jennie had just qualified as a Kinesiologist in 2014 when she first heard about Pranic Healing. Her friend Colm, whom she had met through Kinesiology College, had gone on to study Pranic Healing.

He asked Jennie to attend a meditation session that he was facilitating as part of his training, but she was busy with her small children at the time and was unable to attend.

A few months went by and Jennie found out that Colm was doing a workshop in a local hotel and decided it would be nice to call in to see him. When she got there, she saw what he was doing and thought it looked quite interesting. He explained how Pranic Healing works and how he works on energy blockages to help the body heal itself and then he offered her a treatment session.

Jennie told me, "I wasn't sure what to expect but I wanted to experience what this was all about. He worked on me for around 10 mins and I couldn't believe what had happened when he had finished."

Jennie sat for the treatment session. Colm sprayed his hands with purified water and proceeded to move his hands around her body in a sweeping motion, without physically touching her.

Jennie added, "I had fallen days before, while I was watering flowers and my body was tender all over. After the session, the pain completely disappeared. I was poking myself in all the prior tender parts in disbelief, but there was no pain anywhere. I decided then, that I would like to know more and I started my Pranic Healing training the following year."

Jennie practiced other energy healing therapies in the past but was impressed by how the Pranic Healing modality puts a large focus on self-protection and energy hygiene, which is beneficial to both the client as well as the practitioner. Salt water and purified water (water mixed with isopropyl alcohol and lavender) cleanses the practitioner as well as the energy. She says that there are similarities between Pranic Healing and other energy therapies (as it is all the 'same energy' force), referenced by different names depending on the modality to which you are referring. Prana is the Sanskrit word for the energy or 'life force' transmitted during Pranic Healing.

Pranic Healers use Universal energy rather than the body's own energy to help cleanse undesired viruses that may be causing something as simple as a cold or flu, more serious ailments such as cancer, or psychological problems. Jennie liked that Pranic Healing has a specific protocol for each ailment. There is a Pranic Healing protocol book that contains all the protocols for each disease. Jennie remembers protocols off by heart. There are distinct levels and types of Pranic Healing practiced depending on the severity of the problem. For example, there is a different approach when working with psychological issues as opposed to problems in the physical body. The gentlest energy is always applied when working with children.

Jennie first uses her skills to scan the body and take note of the energies that are having an effect... "it's like listening with your hands." If she sees that there may be a serious energy blockage or that the client complains of more serious symptoms then she would first advise them to speak to their GP. Pranic Healing is a complimentary healing approach that will work alongside any medical diagnosis, but the client must be aware that both can work together simultaneously, for the most favourable outcome. There have been times where Jennie has seen and advised a client about a particular energy effect on the body and the GP has confirmed it with medical testing. There have also been occasions where she has seen small energy changes that are unconfirmed medically and therefore, she can work on these before they manifest into a larger problem.

As a rule, sweeping over the body and replacing the energy is performed while the client is present, but the energy works just as well distantly. There are many different techniques that are used depending on the complaint and these techniques have been tried and tested by many different practitioners over a long period of time, but most importantly by the founder of Pranic Healing, Master Choa Kok Sui.

Master Choa Kok Sui spent 30 years studying all the different energy healing modalities. While working as a chemical engineer in the Philippines, he developed a keen interest in energy medicine and with the help of his spiritual teachers, he developed a simplistic system that everyone can learn, to help heal themselves and their loved ones. Even children can understand its basic concepts.

Jennie's children have grown up using Pranic Healing as their 'go to' First aid tool kit. They would often ask Jennie for Pranic Healing for everyday childhood complaints such as cuts, bites, sores, twisted ankles, as they realised that it could help them heal. There were also times where Jennie witnessed the children doing Pranic Healing on themselves as it was something they were so familiar with; it became a natural habit.

Over the years, Jennie has witnessed amazing healing. One healing that sticks out in her mind is when a teenage boy received severe burns to his face. Jennie stated: "Last year I met a lady I know and she seemed very upset. She told me that her son was melting metal in the shed and it splashed up and hit him in the face so he was going to need a skin graft and there would be scarring. So, I started working on him straight away and a couple of weeks later the lady called me to say that he had gone into get his skin graft, but her son no longer needed it!"

Jennie still practices Kinesiology alongside Pranic Healing and she feels that both can complement each other effectively. Pranic Healing appears to speed up the healing process and the results speak for themselves, often after only one or two sessions. Jennie says: "A lady I saw once, suffered from debilitating migraines for several years. I did the migraine protocol on her only once and she hasn't had a migraine since!"

Being able to do the healing distantly also has huge benefits, especially when it is an animal that needs help. Jennie recently helped a lame sheep and has often worked on pets.
As well as healing individual ailments, another important part of Pranic Healing is the 'Twin Hearts Meditation'.
The Twin Hearts meditation, developed by Master Choa Kok Sui, was developed to help both individuals and humanity collectively to heal… "Just as Pranic Healing can miraculously cure simple and severe ailments; Meditation on Twin Hearts, when practiced by large numbers of people can miraculously heal the entire earth—thereby making the earth more peaceful and harmonious.
"Meditation on Twin Hearts[vi] is one of the most powerful meditation tools for spiritual development. It is a true gift from the great ones"—Grand Master Choa Kok Sui.
https://pranichealingireland.ie/twin-hearts-meditation/ N.D

The Twin Hearts Meditation works on two of the energy centres (chakras): the Heart and Crown. It is a twenty-two-minute meditation that has amazing healing benefits, practiced daily by experienced Pranic Healers. There are monthly meditation practices that occur all over the world, facilitated by qualified Pranic Healers.

Once a month, Jennie facilitates one of these meditations in the local community. They welcome any adult over 18 years old, whether they have experience in Pranic Healing or not. Healing energy is generated by each group meditation and sent out to heal the world. There is no charge to attend these monthly meditations but there is always a collection for a local charity if anyone wishes to donate.

Master Choa Kok Sui always put a huge focus on giving to those who are worse off than us. In 2002, he established the MCKS Charitable Foundation that provides financial assistance to worthwhile Charities. Jennie has presented cheques to local charities to help them stay up and running, she recently presented a cheque to the local soup kitchen.

It was amazing to talk to Jennie about what she does and I realised that there is so much more to Pranic Healing than I initially thought. Its popularity is growing as more people see the benefits that it can bring, and the positive impact it has on the community. Even though Jennie is based in Ireland, there are Pranic Healers based all over the world so there is the possibility of a Twin Hearts Meditation or therapist available somewhere near you.

AUTHOR BIOGRAPHY—Rachel Moir

Rachel has enjoyed writing since an early age. She first loved fictional writing, but as time went by, her passion transpired to telling real life stories. She has heard many accounts of peoples traumas and triumphs and realised that these stories often transfer into stories of hope and inspiration.

Rachel recently published her children's book, Lulu, which is now available on Amazon.

She lives in Ireland in a small, picturesque village in the south of the country and has been married to Conor since 2020. She has four children, Heather, CJ, Laura and Ruby, who are her everyday inspiration.

No Matter how in Control I thought I was, God was about to Show Me Different

By Serena Lange

"Everything that you encounter in life is an important piece of a complex puzzle. You mould the clay. It makes you, you! Every crack in the art just adds to the beauty."
—Sarah Nobody

Before I relate my story, I would like you to close your eyes. I want you to remember a time in your life when things were simple.

A time when you were small... and when the whole world was in front of you. A time when you knew how to dream. A time when there was mystery.

And then the world happened. Like a part to a car that needs to be refinished, your dreams were placed into a box and sand blasted. Each experience a grain of sand that scratched away at that innocence. Just as sand in an hourglass falls the sand in that box took little pieces of you. One grain of sand at a time. You don't know if you like the box with the sand blasting you so hard, but there does not seem to be an exit that can set you free. Just like all the other boxes next to yours, you let the world and the sand shape you. You forget how to dream, how to see you still have the whole world in front of you. The box that at this point feels like living in a hot desert with nothing but wind and sand, can be escaped only when you make the choice to realize that sandstorms can make beauty.

Matthew 17:20
He replied, "Because you have so little faith. Truly I tell you, if you have faith as small as a mustard seed, you can say to this mountain, 'Move from here to there', and it will move. Nothing will be impossible for you."

I once was a little girl who dreamed of being a princess in a land faraway. I wanted a nice house that I would make a home. I wanted a man who loved me with every ounce of who he is. I wanted to grow with that person, laugh with that person, and have a family with them. I wanted what everyone wants: Love.

THE POSITIVE ATTITUDE: SUCCESS LIVING IN SELF LOVE

I found a great guy. We loved one another and had the magnificent blessing of a little boy. I felt as though my life was everything I had ever dreamed in those previous and younger years. I felt that in the game of time, the sand was shaping me in a way that I had always seen in my future. I loved being a mom, and more kids followed. The guy that was great had flaws, but so did I. Onward, I proceeded down the path that I had dreamed. Every time I thought anything different, I tackled it like the biggest linebacker on a football team. Was life easy? No, but whatever came my way would meet the very same fate as any negative thought. Then when I least expected it, baby number four came along—a beautiful little girl. My life was complete. My dream found from a distant memory.

Each day had its own set of challenges. Rather it is the house, laundry, dishes, or helping to shape the minds of these beautiful blessings that called me Mommy. I became too tired for dreams; heck sleep became non-existent. I felt so tired, tired of everything. Every grain of sand in my storm of life felt like a skinned knee with peroxide. I was trying so hard to make everything happen that in turn, I forgot to keep my eyes open for me. I forgot about anything outside of the mundane.

When my face went numb above my left lip I thought nothing of it. I figured I was just getting a cold sore, especially because I was so busy with life and burning the candle at both ends (and that always will result in some kind of disaster).
No matter how in control I thought I was, God was about to show me different.

At this stage in my story, my health care coverage was non-existent. Although my husband worked at the same company for over ten years, health care was only an offered option for him. Working two jobs, he would leave us at 6am and return, after more than his fair share of work, around midnight. Even to consider the idea of the cost and burden I would lay on him to need an appointment, was not something I was willing to do. Consider having to haul four kids to the doctor..., no thanks! And so, I just kept on keeping on.

I continued to do what I did best: not worry and hold it all together. I didn't even tell anyone about my face being numb. No cold sore had shown up and it felt as though I had just been to the dentist. As if the numbing agent was beginning to wear off but prevalent more in some areas than others. I paid it no mind. I was too busy to worry and way too busy to go to a doctor when I had no insurance or funds to pay for a visit, so life continued. The stress was piling up almost faster than the laundry.

One day, while I was trying to keep up with the daunting task of the laundry, I received a call from a friend. We were talking about life as we often did. He had raised his kids and was often a great sounding board for the aches of growing a family. As we chatted and I switched the clothes from one machine to another, I let out a cry of dissatisfaction. He immediately was concerned and asked what was wrong. I proceeded to tell him how it was nothing. His response was, "Sure doesn't sound like anything. Talk to me and tell me what is going on." I proceeded to explain how I was just aggravated with the numb sensation in my face. He asked how long this had been a thing. I felt a shocked silence from over the phone when I said, "I don't know, like a month or maybe two." He was now in a frantic state of concern. He was afraid I was having a stroke or some other health crisis, maybe a heart attack. I slightly may have suggested he was being dramatic. Especially when he told me I needed to go to the emergency room. I literally laughed as I did a self-assessment. I told him how I had no difference in face, arm, or other motor skills. I didn't have slurred speech or chest pain. "Just a little numbness. I think I am getting a cold sore. Plus, I don't have insurance or money to go to the doctor, especially for nothing!". This did not reassure him. He told me I had a week, and either I made an appointment, or he was making it and taking me himself. Obviously concerned, he hung up and I went about my business. As the end of the week approached, I changed my mind about how serious it could be and called the doctor's office. I made an appointment with the nurse practitioner; I mean nothing serious anyway, so better not to bother the actual doctor.

My Mom came over to keep an eye on my kids so I could go. I had underplayed the whole thing to not just my friend, but to my husband, family, and myself.

I went to the appointment. When Sara entered the room, she asked what I was being seen for. I told her no big deal really, just some face numbness. I proceeded to tell her I was going to be responsible for the bill for the visit. I asked her to treat me in a non-invasive way, so it would not break the bank. She graciously agreed and proceeded with the usual dog and pony show—heart, lungs, ears… you know the drill. She asked if I was concerned about anything else, and I responded, "nope." She asked if it was okay to step out and consult with her team. I said, "of course." I was still wondering how much it was going to cost me and how dumb it was to be wasting anyone's time.

She left the room and I waited. When she came back, she told me she believed I had a pinched nerve in my neck. She was going to prescribe me some steroids to help with the inflammation that was possibly occurring, to make the numbness go away. She included very specific instructions: if the numbness did not resolve by Monday, I would need to let her know. She would then have no choice but to order an MRI. The numbness had to be completely gone or an MRI would be needed. I thought, deal! Still stuck in my brain about the cost, but yup, going to take these pills and everything will go back to normal with no need to call.

I could not hear the sand kicking up, nor the wind direction changing. Again, all part of the box of life. The storm was just beginning and I had no idea what was on the horizon.

I took my pills, and the laundry was still getting done. The kids were still learning and loving me. Life as I knew it was continuing to plan... until Monday came and I realized that although the numbness had gotten better, it had not fully resolved. I knew the instructions that I needed to follow. However, wasn't an MRI kind of overkill? I proceeded to call Sara at the doctor's office. She had them order the MRI. Still in the back of my mind was only the inconvenience and the fear of cost. I went to the appointment for the test. I still really had not said anything to anyone and was still convinced of the inconvenience of it all. As I prepared to go into this machine, I for just a moment thought of the potential seriousness of the situation. I think what really made me realize the weight was when the MRI prep began. They had me flat on the table. They put my head in what I can only describe as a head vice. They didn't want me to move at all. Next, they added a giant cage-like contraption. It not only reminded me of the Hannibal Lecter mask (so he would not bite people), but also a deep-sea diver mask. I exclaimed, "why is all this necessary to get pictures of my neck?" It was at that point my whole life and perspective changed. I was informed that they were not looking at my neck, but my head, as in pictures of my brain. You know the whole everything to one's body, the very computer that runs absolutely everything? That's what I thought was the longest hour of my life. I was wrong again.

The only thing that made that hour scan seem so much worse, was the waiting for results. The wonder as to why they were looking at my brain if I had a pinched nerve in my neck. They said it would take about a week to hear back from my doctor. I couldn't sleep or breathe. I felt I could hear every grain of sand running loose from my timer, as if it had been smacked with a giant hammer. This was not going to work so after about two days, I called the hospital and asked that they fax the results to my doctor right away.

The scans are all read by radiology usually within the first day. What takes the most time is the actual process of typing and getting the reports all to the right location. I called the doctor's office and had to wait again. Sara had to review the report and give them permission to tell me what it contained.

After a brief time that felt like centuries, the nurse returned. It went like this: "Great news, there aren't any tumors! But...". Then the other shoe dropped and the sandblaster of life dug me deep. "We need to refer you to a neurologist. We believe that you might have MS". I had no words, I froze. As the air slowly came back to me, I muttered the words, "MS?". I took another breath. In my mind I had heard this term thrown around when talking about celebrities, rarely. I had no idea what it was or what this meant for my future. "What is MS?" I asked. The answer as

I could feel my life changing was as follows: "Have you ever seen the inside of an extension cord?" I responded with, "Yes!" He continued to explain. "The outside of the extension cord is like your central nervous system. It protects all the smaller cords and wires on the inside. When you have MS the body attacks itself and takes small bites out of that cord. Those "bites" create a break down in the communication between your brain and whatever task where the "bite" is. For example, if it was on a nerve where you are trying to lift your arm, it may take longer to lift your arm. In some cases, the connections can be severed completely when the "cord" is completely broken. This would make it so maybe you can no longer lift your arm, because the signal cannot get through."

I must have stayed silent for what seemed to me like forever because he said, "Hello, did I lose you?" I responded with "yes I am still here." Realistically in my mind I was on a whole different planet thinking about all the terrible things that could happen from this point on.

He asked if he could get the referral set up, and I reluctantly in all my fear and terror said "yes".

After I hung up the phone, time seemed to stand still. I caught a quick breath from the drowning reality that was in front of me and did what no one should ever do... I consulted with Dr. Google. This is a term I often refer to as googling any medical 'anything' really. I absolutely advise against this idea. Doctors have medical degrees for a reason and google does not... also for good reason. All the scary things that popped up on my phone screen could put the fear of God into a rock, let alone a human with a heartbeat. I began to see my life flashing before my eyes. In my twenties with four kids, one of whom was only two. I thought, how on God's green earth is my husband going to raise these kids alone? How is he going to react to the news?

I know that when everyone gets married they say, "In sickness and in health", like we are joining the number one cult in the world—marriage. Does anyone really think hard about that as they take those vows? Even then I am pretty sure at such a young age, no one thinks to have issues. I mean that stuff is for your senior years... right? My kids, what about them? How do you tell small children that you have a debilitating disease? One that has high chances of leaving you disabled, cognitively impaired or worse. My mind raced faster than a car on the Autobahn. I again was crying and finding it hard to breathe.

That was the moment I did what I had been taught to do as a child. Something that never leaves you, but somehow as you grow may get put on a back shelf in your mind... I talked to God.

It all began with what you would guess: "Why me?" then it led to: "How?" Eventually bringing me back to the idea of how God will talk back to me. In the back of my 'earth shattered' mind, I knew his word was how he talked. I found my Bible, and immediately was in tears, and before I even opened it I said, "God I am so heart broken. I have no idea what way is up, how to get my bearings, or how to take another breath, let alone step. I need you to talk to me!" With that statement I opened my bible to the most random location.

His words jumped out at me like a tiger from the thick. The message was clear, and his answer was as follows:

Luke 17:5-6
'The apostles said to the Lord, "Increase our faith!" He replied, "If you have faith as small as a mustard seed, you can

say to this mulberry tree, 'Be uprooted and planted in the sea,' and it will obey you. (NIV)

This may not seem like much to most. However, to me it was exactly what I needed to breathe, to take the next step. My tears began to dry. My mind's thoughts immediately changed direction, like shifting wind. Rather than all the negatives, all I could think of was this advice. Maybe a little context would help. A mustard seed is the smallest of seeds. Yet it produces a massive tree with shade for many. God was telling his apostles that they didn't need more faith. That even the absolute tiniest amount, even as small as a mustard seed, holds all that you could ever need.

I could feel the elephant that felt like it was sitting on my chest, stand up. The weight was leaving my shoulders and body. I knew in my heart, that no matter how bad a day may be, and even in the worst moments, I had faith the size of a mustard seed.

So as the story unfolds, I decided that knowledge was power. I took every opportunity I could to read and study Multiple Sclerosis. I wanted to know the disease, know what my doctor may speak with me about, know why certain tests may be required and so much more. My brain became an encyclopedia of information on the topic. I read books from nurses, and anything else that was reputable. I went to lunches hosted by charities and pharmaceutical companies. Anything I could to start the fight that may be in front of me. I refused to go down without a fight.

Then that fateful day came—my referral appointment. I went to a specialist called a neurologist. They deal in brain matters and of course Multiple Sclerosis. After this doctor had reviewed my test results and scans, he came up with the idea that I "may have"

THE POSITIVE ATTITUDE: SUCCESS LIVING IN SELF LOVE

MS. He wanted to wait six months and see if I had any further issues. At that time, he might consider some medication. This however being an isolated issue, he wanted to wait. He also said that a spinal tap could be done but may not give us answers and doesn't always. So, I decided not to let a doctor electively poke around my spine, especially for more maybe's. However, after this appointment, I felt somehow slighted. It didn't really give me the answers that I so badly needed to keep moving forward. My gut told me how everything I had read, and learned so far, was not lining up with this idea. Every part of me questioned the idea I was being fed by this doctor. However, we are programmed to believe the medical professionals who are caring for us.

I had just begun to tell very few people about my diagnosis. My very closest family and husband were the only ones I felt comfortable enough with whom to share my journey. I didn't want people to look at me differently or treat me with kid gloves. I still wanted then to see me, and in all my fears the number one thing I didn't want to do was lose me. I had even decided that I was not going to tell my kids, because it is my job to worry about them, not the other way around. I didn't want them to ever make choices of worrying about their mom because MS would take plenty, but it would never take their innocence, or childhood.

When I was talking to my bonus mom (to most this would be their mother-in-law. However, mine is amazing and I love her so much, so she is a bonus from God), she offered me her suggestion. A light came on at that time. She suggested that if I was questioning anything, maybe a second opinion may be in order. I had never even thought of that. To second guess a doctor was never a real thing, was it? She told me that with a big diagnosis it never hurt to get a second set of eyes. It is life altering after all.

At this moment I did not realize the profound connection we had but felt the divine connection that had been made. For a reason yet to be known to me, it led me in the direction of calling my primary care.

When they answered the phone my request seemed so simple: "I need to be referred to a neurologist, please." The receptionist told me how the computer said I already had been. Time froze again, but only for a second. See, I had not thought any farther than the idea of the request. I took a breath and answered back, "yes, but I would like a second opinion, please."

I am sure she could hear the insecurity in my voice, the not knowing. She then advised me that she would have the doctor call me back.

As my journey with "maybe" MS continued, I felt the roadblocks being built. It was like road construction in the spring living in Michigan. Orange barrels and closed roads pop up more often than the flowers. Quicker too! Time seemed to have yet again taken a slow and stale approach. However, no matter what, I just reminded myself of that mustard seed faith. That faith is believing not necessarily seeing.

Then the phone rang.

On the other end I found my amazing provider. She was wondering what was going on and how she could help. I began to explain how I felt the doctor had a more "Old School" approach and I didn't necessarily feel confident in his findings. I told her how it felt to contradict all the things I had read. One of those things being to treat MS as soon as you suspect it, to not wait for more issues. If the treatment happens within the first year of diagnosis, then it vastly decreases your chances of disability. I also told her with big things a second set of eyes, never hurts. She agreed with me and was happy to refer me to someone she had worked with during her residency. She would put in the referral and if I needed anything else, not to hesitate. At that moment I felt like a wrecking ball had just knocked down one of many walls.

The phone rang and the call from the new referral doctor was in. I had an appointment and again, time seemed to freeze. Funny how if you don't want time to fly by, it is faster than light. When you really want it to fly by, a giant coffee or red bull can't make it move. You could electrocute it with 1000 watts and time still would stand still.

The day finally arrived; my second opinion. I went into the doctor; they had all the test results and the same information as the first doctor. They did all my vitals and I waited in anticipation for the doctor. He entered the room, introduced himself and then asked me, "I see you just saw a doctor, so what brings you to my office to see me today?"

You are never prepared to tell a doctor that you are now in front of them because you did not trust the previous doctor.

I took a deep breath and a gulp of air. I began to explain how the other doctor didn't make me feel confident. I cannot live my life with a maybe I have MS and so I thought it best to get a fresh set of eyes on the situation. He looked down at his screen and reviewed the information again, and then looked at me with eyes of confidence. He said, "why did you not have a spinal tap? Did you have blood work done?" I responded to him how it was explained to me that the spinal tap would not likely give me any more answers, so I took a pass on the hole in my spine. He looked at me with concern and said, "in 90% of cases we can definitively diagnose MS with a spinal tap."

I looked at him and filled with anger, yet at the same time felt divine relief. I obviously was not in the right place to start with but could also feel the peace of knowing I was now. However, I was also filled with anxiety because I know this means more waiting and more tests. Being poked at like some cattle being loaded into the paddy wagon was not what I was looking forward to. Other than the test, my patience would be tested waiting on the results.

Moving forward, his suggestion was to proceed with the spinal tap and some blood work. He explained how other things can create MS symptoms. For example, vitamins being unbalanced, or even something like Lyme disease. I decided that being poked probably was not the worst of things, especially if it brought me closure and some answers. I agreed and the tests were ordered. Again, it felt like more walls were being built. As if I lived in a body but had no control. Running through the motions and the sands in the time glass dropping. I felt cornered by so many things beyond my control, at the same time knowing life had to go on. My kids still need their mom and a happy one. I proceeded as normally as possible. Continuing to remind myself of the mustard seed faith I had, as if God himself had angels whispering it in my ears to soothe my soul.

The spinal tap date rolled up on me like a crashing wave. My Sister took me so I could laugh instead of cry. She is always my person who can make my heart smile. Good or bad she loves me and all my crazy, she also tends to keep me calm and not overreact. When we arrived at the hospital, they would not let her come back with me. I could feel the elephant sitting on me yet again, the time dragging. Then, however, I heard the angels whispering the faith of a mustard seed, and I knew God had me, no matter what.

The doctor and nurse prepared me for what I considered another poking. This time it was quite literally just that. They provided me with a pillow and a standard hospital tray. The ones every room has. They adjusted the table to a shorter level. Put the pillow on top and asked me to lean on it. I had to crouch over this table and pillow set up to open my spine spaces. Then they were going to insert a needle into the space and remove some of the fluid that flows to the brain. It was of utmost importance that I did not move at all during this process because that could put the needle in the spine someplace we didn't want it. That could result in paralysis if I remember correctly. Now the elephant felt like it was on my back, and breathing seemed to be difficult… I was frozen. News that made moving feel next to impossible. They filled several vials with my brain juice, drop by drop. Thirty minutes might well have been thirty years. Finally, they told me I can move again… the elephant and weight leave me as time slowly moves by. However, it still was not at full speed because now I need answers. What was all this for if not answers!

At that time, not only did I feel in the world's biggest nightmare but a time warp. It felt as if the appointments would never end and the answers nowhere to be found. I found myself again in the doctor's office with hopes that these tests would give doctor number two some answers.

They called me back to the room. I said a prayer in my head: please may I have some answers, God. My faith is always at least a mustard seed. I felt peace if only for a moment.

The doctor entered the room and his face seemed sombre. "I have some results." Reluctantly I take a deep cleansing breath and say: "let's hear them".

In that very moment he spoke the words I thought that I was ready for, yet you never can be really prepared for: "You definitely have Multiple Sclerosis."

At the same time, I felt that my world was ending. All the walls continued to be built, but then I also decided at that moment, I can't define the diagnosis but I can and will define the verdict. I will be the biggest wrecking ball to any walls, and God will guide me! This is when I became an MS warrior! I will define me and my MS!

Along the way on this new journey that I found myself in, things have been hard at times. You would think that MS would constantly weigh on one's heart and mind. Interestingly, MS has helped me live. There is something about a life altering experience that catalyses you to live. When you have the faith of a mustard seed and you just trust God's plan, you live. The sand in that timer becomes mustard seeds. Every opportunity is seen to bring growth. To plant the same seed and affect the world in a positive way. See you realize on a whole different level how God connects us all. That you need to plant the seed, because he will at some point and time help the tree grow. You even more so see how no one is guaranteed even another second on this planet, so what legacy do you want to leave this world with?

My MS has made every aspect of my life and the glasses I see it through so different. I can show my children that nothing defines you, but you. I have learned that God needs me to be me and nothing else. That means sometimes being vulnerable and

THE POSITIVE ATTITUDE: SUCCESS LIVING IN SELF LOVE

taking that leap of faith with my mustard seed. It has allowed me to ask why not me? Rather than, why me?

Think of anyone in your life that you have ever thought of as your hero. They are not viewed that way because of their homes, cars, or bank accounts. You didn't view them as inspiring because of everything in their life being so perfect. Instead, our heroes are just that, because of the adversity they conquer. If it is Superman even, he conquers the bad guys, he makes good choices to do the right thing, and he makes the right choice in the face of adversity. Superman can only make a good choice because of adversity, because the adversity exists.

I am a better person because of MS! It has given me more than I will ever allow it to take. During my journey I learned of other's journeys. Remember my bonus Mom and how she advised me to get a second opinion? That is because she was at the same time I was having my MS struggle, learning of her breast cancer diagnosis. She too was a warrior, maybe from a different tribe but a warrior! Her battle helped me so much along the way. Even though the diseases are different, the feelings and experiences are so similar. We would often find ourselves talking about doctors, tests, or infusions. Our paths helped one another, and even at our worst, we spread love and light.

A year after being diagnosed, I felt empowered to tell others about my journey. To share the most vulnerable part of myself. I even found the courage to tell my children. I was amazed by how they themselves became advocates for MS. They began to educate people along their journeys. By letting those around me in, I saw a whole sea of love embrace me. I stood in God's light, just how he made me. Vulnerable while at the very same time wearing his armor and being a warrior. It allowed those around me to see the struggle, but more importantly the struggle that leads to the triumph. It helped me to not fear failure but to embrace it. To see failure, bad days, setbacks as an opportunity to get back up, dust it off, look for a new opportunity and try again. I became a better problem solver, parent, wife, daughter, and person because of how MS helped to shape me. Never forgetting that even on my worst day, I always have at least the faith of a mustard seed. Some of the most beautiful art in the universe is seen that way because of its flaws. God made me perfectly imperfect!

When you find yourself in that moment, in your defining moment, make a choice to have that faith. Faith of a mustard seed! Know that God and you will make beauty from the ashes! That even if it doesn't seem like it at that moment, you are putting on your armor and you are going to live the best version of you! Caterpillars do not turn into butterflies overnight! You are a warrior and someone's hero! You have got this!

Today's thoughts:

MS
I did not ask for you today,
I did not ask for you any day,
I do not want the shakes and quakes,
I do not want the fatigue either... by the way.
I do not want the needles or the meds
I do not want them, I said!
But you didn't ask me what I thought,
Or when a time would be good for what I want.
You didn't consider my need to get out of bed

Or my need to rest my head.
You did not consider the amount of stress
Or that my aches and pains would not bend.
But guess what MS.,
I have a message for you instead,
I do not care that you didn't ask,
I do not care that you didn't care,
I do not care about the needles,
Matter of fact, the nurses feed me snacks!
I do not care what you say,
Because I am going to do this MY WAY!
I will keep pushing through,
I will keep on pushing you,
Even though I can't make you go,
I will make you bend my way,
I will make you live my way,
Watching me triumph anyway,
Because truth be told,
God is in control,
So, you can't have me, that's what I say,
Because I will fight you every day!
I am me, and you live here
I'm defying my verdict… you hear!!!

Love,
Me 🖤
MS kicking bad ass

The Purple Monster Under the Bed

By Serena Lange

Luke 17:5-6
The apostles said to the Lord, "Increase our faith!"
He replied, "If you have faith as small as a mustard seed, you can say to this mulberry tree, 'Be uprooted and planted into the sea,' and it would have to obey you.

Fear is a funny thing. Maybe you have a fear of spiders, or maybe the monster under the bed or maybe social situations. However, usually at some point and time in our lives, we realize that the very thing we feared, was not so bad after all. Life also has a funny way of teaching us that the thing we never thought of or saw as a possible threat can be the scariest thing of all.

When my kids were little I found myself like most moms, scared of the possibility of SIDS, the light socket they may put their fingers in, the tables sharp pointy corners, or germs... oh, the germs. Their complete lack of concern for anything seemed overwhelming and terrifying. Somehow the idea that eating something from under the sink or running into the street in front of a car could kill them, didn't register.

Yet they could fear the monster under their bed.

That was the easy thing to fix. A little talk about how monsters are not real, a prayer for protection and if nothing else, a little monster spray worked wonders. All the time and energy I had spent trying to be the very best Mom I could be, had me missing the purple monster that was lurking under my bed, that I didn't even know existed.

See, while I spent all these years making memories and trying to grow great members of society, I did not know the storm that was brewing. My village that has helped me raise my kids has always been nothing but the best. On my worst days they can shine light into places I had no idea still could find light. Even as I sit here and type this story, it is a light that shines on a dream I thought had long passed, by an amazing friend.

My Mom was always one of my biggest supporters in my village. She gave each of my children a cute animal nickname. She held them, read them stories, and did things that only the very best Nana's do. She would sit at sporting events, and listen to all their adventures, along with the horror stories of their 'so unfair' Mom. She could make anything better and turn tears into laughter. She even would be a great reminder to the village Queen that the sun would again rise, and these things that seem so impossible today, will be the things you miss someday. She was a superhero, with supernatural powers of calming.

At that time, I didn't realize she was giving me valuable advice, wisdom beyond my years, to eventually fight the purple monster under the bed.

As my children grew, so did my village and the only thing I found I lacked was time. As they grew the worries changed, but as a mom your worries for your children will never be vanquished.

Their Nana has always been such a strong force, until one day she became more distant. She seemed to want to be less involved in all the things she once had. We noticed that she was becoming more emotional. She found so many things to be irritating or took so much more to heart. Her laughter began to dwindle, and her hobbies became non-existent.

One day we were all at my house playing cards. We were playing a game that she had taught me when I was young. Her and her friends would always play cards, so into my teen years, my friends and I learned. We would often have card nights with all the adults and teens playing together. I wanted to be sure this was part of my kids village, so when Nana came over it was time to hang out and play. We all sat around the table, joking, and laughing. However, Nana found herself struggling to keep up. She at times seemed to struggle to speak. She had a hard time counting and following the game. I thought to myself maybe it was just me.

After talking to others in private, they too had noticed the difficulty she was having. This is when I learned that while I was managing the village of life and kids, a purple monster I should have feared, had been hiding under the bed.

Not wanting to become too alarmed, I reached out to the doctor's office and asked if they had dementia as a diagnosis code in my mom's chart. The answer was yes, they do. I then asked them if the chart said why that was? They said that it did not. I then asked if there was a protocol? Shouldn't there be some follow up if one decides to code a patient's chart with dementia? I then asked if she had a follow up appointment?

You see, my mom had been considered borderline diabetic for some time. To be sure that they stayed on top of her disease, she usually had to do blood work and follow up every three months. They advised me that she was coming in soon for her follow up. I did not want to take anything away from my mom or make her feel like she was not making her own choices. I requested that when she came into the office for her follow up that they reviewed the idea of memory issues and refer her to a specialist. They told me they would note the chart so that it would be followed up. [I knew that if they referred her to a specialist she would ask me to take her. This way she still has control but we can also get things investigated].

Mom's doctor's appointment came around, and nothing. I called the office back and asked if it had been investigated and a referral made. They told me there were not even notes from speaking with me. I was livid to say the least! I said, "that is enough, she needs a referral to a neurologist!". They assured me that they would get on it and be sure that the follow up would happen. I waited as I began to realize that all this time there was a "monster under my bed". Something I should have been afraid of, been paying closer attention to, but failed to know it even existed.

THE POSITIVE ATTITUDE: SUCCESS LIVING IN SELF LOVE

Weeks went by, and I continued to check in on my mom. See, we have this amazing relationship and would talk almost every day. When I talked to her I found that work and everyone there had been bothering her. She felt like they were saying she didn't know how to do her job. They would say she didn't do things that she insisted she had. She just thought that maybe they wanted someone else to do her job and were looking for reasons to make that happen. My Mom had worked for this company for over 33 years. I knew she knew how to do her job.

She worked better with kids than adults. However, changes became harder for her to accept and each time I began to speak with her, she was mad at work. Out of nowhere she decided that it was time to quit, and without warning she put in her two weeks' notice. This gave me the opportunity to have a talk I never even knew I needed. I explained with a frog in my throat, and a crack in my heart… "Mom", I said, "if you feel that work is going so bad and you are struggling this much, maybe we need to go see the doctor?". She agreed and claimed she was going to ask me to make an appointment.

It had now been weeks with no word from the doctor's office, leaning on months. I called the office and told them the whole thing, how I had been reaching out and nothing had been done. It was unacceptable! I demanded a referral to a memory care neurologist, and I gave them a name. I told them they had till the end of business to call me back and let me know it had been done. I explained my mom had now quit her job because of the issues, while they let her fall through the cracks!

By the end of the day, I had my mom's referral, and the journey to learn about "the monster under my bed" began. I had no idea what this thing was. I was so scared of this thing that was hurting my mom, but I sought out to find answers and slay the fear just like I vanquished monsters before it, under my kids beds.

The appointment had been made, and I knew my mom was in the best of hands because I went to this doctor's office full of Neurogenesis for my own care. I had been fighting multiple sclerosis for years at this point. I knew the very best care, technology and abilities were at the hands of these very doctors. The team of medical professionals here was on the cutting edge of all the latest and greatest, so I knew she would find the monster that was hurting my mom.

My mom was nervous and so was I. We entered this appointment with the idea we may find some answers. During this time, my mom had returned to work on a substitute basis. She had missed all the kids so much, so she wanted to do less but still be involved. It had been going great so far. I thought to myself as we sat in this doctor's office maybe I had been overreacting. Maybe this was just normal... she is getting older. However, my self-doubt continued to creep in, and the fear began to swell.

The doctor came in. She was so kind and light-hearted. I am not sure how because my heart was racing almost as fast as my mind. She talked to us and asked what had been going on and ordered several tests to try and find out everything she could, that way we could beat this faceless monster. These tests included blood work and an MRI.

When we returned to the doctor after all the test results had come in, she had some clues as to what may be happening. The MRI revealed that there were several small bleeds that had healed in her brain. Her blood test also showed elevated amlodipine numbers that would account for the brain bleeds and could be a reason for her recent struggles. However, because of these results she would like to run one more test... a spinal tap. The doctor told us that these could also be signs of Alzheimer's disease but could also not be as well. Nowadays a spinal tap can definitively give you a diagnosis in 98% of cases. Even though we were both nervous, we agreed to the test.

I am now beyond scared. They are talking about putting a needle into my mom's spine. They are talking about her someday not knowing me. I fought back the tears and anxiety. I assured my mom that no matter the answers we would fight this monster together, just like the ones from my childhood and my kids' youth.

On the day of the test, we were both nervous. To help calm our nerves, we showed up to the hospital a little early. Of course, we decided some retail therapy may help. We walked into the gift shop there as we waited and found the most adorable things. Stuffed animals that had calming lavender and chamomile. You can even put them in the microwave to make them warm packs. We both looked at the adorable pink flamingo, and the sloth.

Mom's name was called and it was time to go. I assured her it would all be okay. I described the procedure to her, and that I too had one done. It would be a little uncomfortable, but nothing to fear. They gave her some meds to make her relax. She began joking with the nurses and had the whole pre op room laughing. As they wheeled her away, all my greatest fear that I never even knew I had, began to swirl like a giant wave crashing over me.

I went back to the gift shop as I waited. I saw those cute critters still sitting there. That is when I knew they had to come home with us. Just like when I was a kid a stuffed animal could make almost anything better, and it sure did. As she woke up in the recovery room I was there waiting with her flamingo. Her smile was as big as the pacific, at that moment. Instead of this monster we needed to fight, all we could do is feel the love in the room. From that moment on those "warmies" became our coping mechanism as we fought the monster under our bed, together.

I prepared for the worst as we waited to find out the results. I felt in my heart I knew the face of this monster was purple, and its name was Alzheimer's. However, I kept hope alive that I was wrong, praying deeply in those moments to help lift the weight. As the days seemed to grow longer, and it seemed months had passed, time seemed to move slower than a snail. I increasingly became impatient as I waited to give my monster a face and name.

Finally, I decided to call and have the test results mailed to me, because that would be faster than waiting on the appointment. Even though it was faster, it still seemed like decades.

Eventually the letter came. I sat and stared at it. I could not decide if I really wanted answers as the fear and anxiety washed over me. I suddenly felt like the waves were unbearable and I could not keep my head above water. Struggling to breathe, I looked to God, took a deep breath, and then I opened the letter. It was a situation that you think you are prepared for, yet there is no way to truly ever be prepared.

In the envelope I uncovered the monster that had been hurting my mom, and everyone who loves her. I found the monster under the bed's face and color. I found out it was a purple monster known as Alzheimer's!

In that moment my eyes filled with tears of sadness but also happiness. The happiness was to finally be able to give it a name and a face. The sadness is for obvious reasons. She would never again be the mom I had known before. Now what to do? Do I tell her? Wait till the appointment? Do I tell my dad? What are the next steps? So many more questions when I thought I was finding answers. I reminded myself to take the advice I have given so many other people. The same advice my mom had given me as I grew. One step at a time.

I decided that if someone knew important information about me, I would want to know. So, I put one foot in front of the other, I sat my mom down and I told her that she had Alzheimer's.

We cried together as she told me she just knew. I said "don't worry Mom, we love you and we will all fight this together! One step at a time. Even though there is no cure, we will put every roadblock that we can in its way. Just like with my MS. It will all be okay mom!" I assured her. We just hugged and took it all in. Next step is the actual doctor's appointment.

We returned to the doctor and she gave us an official diagnosis, just as we had planned. We asked what the next steps were. The answers were some of what we expected and things that we never thought of. My mom needed to continue the medicine she had been taking already. They were going to add one more med for memory retention to hopefully help things work as well as they could for as long as they could. We were on board with that.

Then the other footstep felt like a kick in the groin. She needed to stop driving. Under no circumstances was she to drive. We discovered Alzheimer's messes not just with memory but with depth perception. They also told us how she was at the middle stages of the disease already, based on the testing. She also could no longer work. Not even as a sub. In the blink of an eye my mom and how she had defined herself for her whole life, had ended. She had her independence stolen from her. No more cooking, driving, kids, working and she was heartbroken.

The only pain worse than your own is when the people you love more than anything, are in pain and you can do nothing. The car ride home was heavier than a wall of bricks and more silent than the night air. When we got home, I asked her if she needed me to call her boss and let her know. In tears she said yes. I had to put in her resignation from the thing that defined her, after 35 years. No celebrating or party, just tears. We became a part of a community no one ever wants to be a part of. This purple monster that had grown under my bed was scarier than anything I thought I could ever face as a kid. No monster spray could cure it.

What is the silver lining you may ask? The answer is that it was a realization that God's plan is far more advanced or in tune than our own. I could not have helped my mom the same way I did without having MS. The thing that at one time I thought was a curse was in this case a blessing. I had gone through so many of the tests my mom had. It allowed me experience and wisdom beyond my years. It helped me empathize and provide comfort only I could. It let me be a magnificent medical advocate. It let me know where to get the very best care. My monster helped me to know how to find my moms, how to give it a face, how to tame it as best we can.

You see there is power in your struggle. The journey you tread can help others through their journey. You must find joy in the journey. God's plan will ultimately always be better even when it seems like you are drowning. Find your village and add to it. Count on those who can help you on the journey. I have found the most amazing people at the least expected times in the strangest of places. We are all just spinning on this big dirty rock, around a ball of fire, so let's make it beautiful. You see, the perfection is never where you find the beauty, it is in the perfectly imperfect. Although the purple monster will always be under the bed, I have decided to not be afraid. I have decided God would want me to be at peace with it, give it some grace, and share my sandwich.

May you find the same strength as you fight the monsters under your bed! Give yourself grace and share your sandwich.

AUTHOR BIOGRAPHY—Serena Lange

Serena uses the pen name Sarah Nobody, a biblical reference to Sarah. Serena's long held dream has always been to become an author but did not realise her dream until much later in life. Serena credits her success to God. She is a Multiple Sclerosis Warrior who was diagnosed in June of 2014. She is a mom to three amazing boys and a girl.

Serena's husband was her high school sweetheart and they have been together for two decades. They live on a hobby farm in Michigan, along with chickens, goats, a sheep, dogs, and cats. In her spare time, Serena supports her kids in many sports and coaches cheer. She enjoys being an active part of her community and making the world better with kindness and love.

Serena is also a caregiver to her mother who has been diagnosed with Alzheimer's. Her goal in life is to leave a mark on this world that will have a lasting impact. She looks forward to continuing to write and inspire future generations.

In Search for Meaning: Listening to the Guidance from Inner Self

By Karen Tants

Life moves us ever onward.
We start out with ideals; some realistic, some seemingly impossible to achieve. We think we know what we want from life and love. Yet, life often pulls the proverbial rug out from under us... "That's what YOU think", says Life. And throws challenges here, there, and everywhere.

But that's precisely where we experience the 'silver linings'. Often that 'positivity and self-loving', healing path guides us down to dark places before we come out the other side stronger, more resilient, with the ability to see the bigger picture, and with new awareness of why life happens as it does.

It is from that darkness that we find our inner light, switch it on and light the way. It becomes a path of Self-discovery.

My experiences have taught me that when we become consciously aware of Self and what we 'put out' into the world, we act as our own catalyst. Sometimes the catalyst is a response to certain stimuli, a 'calling', or the result of negative experiences, events, or debilitating illness either mental or physical that makes us uncomfortable within ourselves: these are all catalysts for healing change. Some catalysts will shake us to the very core of our being to wake us up to a higher purpose, and we begin to question everything.

For me, my catalyst began quietly when I wanted to change and become a better person, not only for myself, but also for my loved ones and others. Wanting to forgive and be forgiven, I discovered the teachings of Ho'oponopono. Interestingly, there was a correlation between my inner growth desire and the opening of my psychic/intuitive awareness, angelic and guidance healing... it is almost like, simultaneously the Spirit/Divine realms came to meet me.

I had already taken responsibility for my part in the drama of life, which led me to become more aware of my need to change how I felt about myself, how others may "receive" me, and I had begun to have thoughts of being an observer, or "witness" of me as if I was outside of myself. This was around 2005 when many life changes were happening... including my youngest starting school, going back to work, and marrying my third husband.

As a result, my spiritual journey began and it felt like I was on fast-forward. I studied the inner realms of spirituality, read books, and attended healing groups and workshops. I was receiving insight, hearing guidance, and seeing visions; including images of Jesus lifting me up and my ex-brother-in-law (who had passed) showing me I was doing the right thing (which meant so much at that time).

Since then, I've had many significant lucid dreams, spiritual visions, and insight beyond what I consciously know or were aware of involving people, places, and situations; mostly either transformative or guiding and teaching me what I needed to know. Later, when I was coming up with ideas for my book titles, I discovered very quickly that the amount of synchronicity I received from (what I thought were) my own ideas that I expected to be unique, were in fact, not unique. This was an important lesson.

What we 'extract' is 'individualised' and perceived differently for all. It is fluid, never still, and different at any given point in time… changing as we do, as we grow in understanding, expansion, and capacity. It is coloured by our beliefs, perceptions, ideals, teachings, indoctrinations, and subconscious thought patterns, memories, and fears.

"*Draw a Beacon*"

In 2005, amidst my 'fast-forward', these words were clearly spoken to me and awoke me from sleep. I didn't understand the meaning at the time, I just knew that they were important in some way. When I woke up the next morning, I blinked facing the white wall of the bedroom. As I opened my eyes I saw a light beam on the wall for a moment, then it was gone. Just like you would shine a torch on an object and when you switch it off the light goes. I was intrigued! I blinked again by closing my eyes tightly and opening them just as quickly; there again, I saw a light beam where my eyes were focused on the wall.

Meaning: At the time, I felt insight was telling me that I have an inner light and that I needed to shine my light to reach out to others and to also be seen and guided. To light my way out of the darkness. To "see" my way forward; like a lighthouse that guides seafarers to find their direction. I knew deep down it likely means so much more than that, and I know that we all have that light within that we can 'draw upon' when needed.

Further to this, I found in my journal (from much later) the following insight I received regarding Beacons at a time when I was delving into Dharma as opposed to Karma, in my musings on dharma work:

Individual Will and Unconscious Creating

There is a part of us (quintessence) that when given up to God (omnipresence) enables us to be a conduit to bring forth and emit goodness, benevolence, freedom from karmic creating and being a force for good in the world and within oneself.

We either draw people to us or repel them. Symptoms of being unaware and ignorant of the effect we have on others, how we are 'felt' by others (how our energy is received), will be evident in the way people react to us. We are a 'repository of learning' and can choose to alter this force by becoming self-aware and teachable. Self-development lifts focus and intent to learn and change.

God's Will over individual will requires acknowledgment of a benevolent higher force and power greater than one's own. Along with the belief that this force works FOR us, not against us. "God always has the last word; let the energy form around that."

Ways and practices to benevolence and peace
- ♥ Prayer and contemplation on God and/or Deities
- ♥ Intent and focus on purpose and destiny
- ♥ Mantras – Mahayana – Meditation
- ♥ Ho'oponopono
- ♥ Service to others

Means
- ♥ Simplify
- ♥ Declutter
- ♥ Self-care
- ♥ Identify self-sabotaging behaviours that block progress
- ♥ Be teachable
- ♥ Willingness to change

Ask

Is God 'In' my way? Or 'The Path'. And will anything change, if "I" don't?

Vision

A sparkling clean wine glass was raised in front of me, it instantly was filled to the rim with water as I watched. A finger of a right hand was placed on the top and gently touched around the top of the glass, on top of the water (not touching the rim) in a circular motion; coloured orbs of light energy emitted onto the top of the glass as it formed a perfect circle.

Next, I 'heard' a sharp tap, and a finger on the rim of the glass, instantly shattering the sides of the glass into a speckled effect yet still holding together. The top of the glass where the circle had been formed was clear, appearing solid, untouched, and unaffected.

My feeling is this vision speaks of wisdom and insight into the magical properties we all contain within to transmute and transform our life experiences. We are an instrument of the divine, and as such, capable of our own self-mastery. We create magic and transmutation that is literally at our fingertips. The wine glass being symbolic of the Alchemist.

Turning water into wine – Blessings of Christ. A chalice of alchemical transmutation. A receptacle (as we are in body).

Thinking of us as instruments of the Divine, we are capable to lift the spirits and bring forth Joy. It is a calling of the Soul to inner resonance with something beautiful and beyond time. It evokes meaning and carries creativity. Nothing is performed alone; everything is channelled and influences all in multitudinous ways dependent solely on our ability to recognise and integrate the signs and messages that are continually around and within us. These signs, messages and insight are fluid, they change as we change… grow as we grow… and they are perfectly "dispensed" for where we are in any given moment in time. They can be the same message delivered in a thousand different ways.

No one is perfect, and we shouldn't aim to be… what we should aim for is a healthy dose of self-love to validate our self and not look for external validation. Live own truth, know that we are loved for being exactly who we are with all imperfections.

Self-love is the proving ground for Unconditional Love. Everything emits from self… so don't leave 'you' out of the equation.

Dr. Wayne Dyer in 'Ambition to Meaning': "Don't die with your music still in you." And as Leonard Cohen sang:

"There is a crack in everything; that's how the light gets in."

AUTHOR BIOGRAPHY—Karen Tants

Karen was born in the UK and emigrated to Australia with her parents and sister in 1976. She is a mother and a grandmother.

Karen is a spiritual self-help writer, ghost-writer, author, and editor who currently works with authors and compilers to become self-published.

The Positive Attitude is Karen's ninth anthology as a co-author and she plans to write her own fifth book in the not-too-distant future.

Karen has a background in healing and is a Usui Reiki and Seichim master practitioner/teacher (since 2006). She has an interest in all healing modalities and integrative therapies.

www.facebook.com/karen.tants
www.facebook.com/intuitiveediting/

You Are Your Own Sunshine

By Geri Magee, Ph.D.

Do you know that famous children's song, "You Are My Sunshine?" My parents sang this song to me as a child. I now sing it to my own children and grandchildren. I was caught many times by my kids (when they were younger) singing it to myself in the mirror while getting ready for work. The kids would make fun of me while singing the song in the car on the way to school.

What they did not know at the time, as a single parent raising three kids plus their friends (who came to visit or predominantly lived at my home), was that I was an example of how I wanted my own life to be. I had to be happy for everyone else to be happy, or so I thought.

Twenty-three years now of working on my co-dependency issues in relationships, I discovered I can't make anyone else feel what they do or do not want to feel. I also found out the reason kids loved to come to my home was that I chose to be happy and had created a positive, safe environment for all, including at times the parents of the children who came over to visit. I went to bed singing the Sunshine song and I woke up singing the Sunshine song. I realize now, looking back, that I created my own sunshine, every day.

I know it wasn't an easy thing to do, day-to-day and yes, I had my moments of deep sorrow and pain, as everyone does in one's life journey. However, I took the opportunity to learn from those times, to make sure I did not repeat the underlying issues and yes, my goal each day was to find the "silver lining" in the cloud throughout most of my unhappy moments. What did I learn from that experience, what did I want to leave behind from that moment in time, and what did I want to take ahead for the future? What I learned from each lesson was to not 'repeat the bad' to see what lesson I learned. However, to also hold onto what was good from the situation and the outcome of it.

As I progressed through life, I kept manifesting this trait of my personality in that I truly became my own sunshine. As I grew, friends, neighbors and family members would nickname me, Sunshine, and I realized that others could see me as a person who brings spiritual light into the world.

Recently, I had someone close to me say: "Why do you always have to be so happy even if shit goes wrong?" As I looked at that person, I truthfully and whole-heartedly said: "Not all of us have to wear the darkest parts of their heart and soul on their face and in their body language." I choose to show the world (or at least Geri's world; those who come and go from my daily life's journey) that I know what hardship is. However, I do not believe it is beneficial to show it all the time especially professionally, believing the old adage's; "leave your worries at home" and "leave your work at the office," have helped me many times.

I survived extremely difficult circumstances in my life; however, I still choose to live by demonstrating the beauty of it all and my heart and soul radiate from the inside out.

I had an experience recently; someone close to me whom I care for considerably was going through multiple situations. His life events came crashing down around him; one wave after another impacted his work, continued education, home life and of course, himself. This person snapped at me and said: "Why are you always so happy and cheerful, are you putting on a fake cheerful face?" I looked and said: "No, I am not. When you have time, I will be glad to sit with you to hear all of what is going on and I will be more than happy to share with you how I get through each day."

Push away from the negative and discomfiting intentions of what others' want you to do or feel. Only YOU can make yourself feel and choose to be proactive rather than reactive in life!

I have learned over the years in my co-dependent recovery that I need to stop for fifteen minutes to disconnect from the negativity, place myself in a safe space, do an internal check-up and look at what is going on inside and around me. I then ask myself: "Who is causing this impact that dampens my light, trying to sabotage me from being the person I choose and want to be?". Also: "Who can aide me during this time of need?". Especially while trying to put life's little puzzle pieces back together again. I ask myself, "when I go back into the toxic environment, what do I hope to change within myself? If possible, can I do action versus reaction, utilizing my inner consciousness and spirit collectively for the best outcome?". "If I cannot change anything in my current system, is there a way to find the resource I need?". "If resources aren't available, what would be the healthiest exit strategy?".

My primary goal is to be as authentic and truthful to myself as possible. I can see myself start to glean, and as I do my light comes out and I try to mindful of those around me when I start this miraculous change in my environment. I ask myself: "How are others in my system reacting to this healthy change I decided to create?".

My best advice is to empower yourself with self-love! Believe me, I know it's not always easy, it can be very painful too. It does feel so much better being aware of who you truly are! The first few steps are hard I know. However, you will see your 'shine' immediately start to come through once you leave the negativity behind you.

Throughout my fifty-plus years of life, I have learned that by choosing to live and view my life in a positive way, each day as often as I can, that it is the innate nature in which I have utilized the law of attraction.

A few weeks later, I saw this person (mentioned above in my life) look happy for the first time in a long time. I said: "Wow! What happened in your life that is so great?". The person said: "How can you tell?" My answer: "It is so obvious on your face, in your body language and I can see your light. How have you been picking up the pieces through all the negativities?" I was told of their past day's events from waking up to moving forward through a super stressful week; further stating: "No matter what is going around me, I am going to find the good in this day! As

I have been, from since we last spoke." They believed they could do it and so, they did!

Not only am I a firm believer in my own life's law of attraction, but I am also witnessing so many others who have accepted their true inner gifts. I have had the privilege to watch as each of them day-by-day makes progress to enlighten themselves and take notice of the power of positivity. They are already sharing it with others, as I am with you as you read this chapter. By watching the law of attraction unfold in another's life journey and by personally experiencing the law of attraction in my own life seeing from my own eyes, my heart and soul feel this immense energy that comes out when applying these actions on my journey.

Now, for the person I spoke of earlier, when they began to glean their own truth and authenticity, others became aware and witnessed their transformation. Doors started to open for them in multiple areas of their life. I am privileged to be a witness to their transformation since they are so important to me. I passionately believe positivity draws positivity and the things that we fret about become life-changing events for us as time goes by.

My friend was able to save his job, move to another division and reap the rewards to allow his soul to shine through, whilst gleaning through the negativity. I must mention; during this time, he made it through multiple events of departmental reorganization, management changes, job changes, layoffs, family member illnesses and passing, plus a lot more than he had on his plate.

While making these personal changes he had no idea how many lives he was able to impact before leaving his division. Now, as a friend, I know this is work-in-progress and just baby steps toward having a happy, fulfilling life. As I still grow, beginning from many years ago, now, they must, too. It is a beautiful gift to be a part of someone else's life, nonetheless.

Here are just a few 'tools' I was shown that have helped me to navigate the experiences of my life, both personally as well as professionally.

1. Write down a list of all the people you love in your world. Now, please do this before proceeding further in this chapter. If, at this moment, you are unable to write for any reason, just think of the people you love.

2. Were you stuck in my theory? Writing things down can help clarify things in your mind and help toward a solution.

3. Look at your reflection in a mirror (your whole self) and say to each part of yourself: "I Love You." This can be a difficult exercise. A therapist told me to do this years ago, it has been successful for myself as well as for others.

4. Now, on your list of loved ones at step 1, what number were you? If you were not there, write your name at the top of the list. Trust me, I did not have myself on my list either a year ago. I now keep this in my bathroom, where I can see it each day. A part of a guiding light's resource is to look at oneself from the inside out.

So, now to share my story of how I learned to glean. There have been several times in my life when I have been in the deepest part of my 'very dark basement of muck' with confusion, regret, stagnation, the list goes on in "Geri's World." Many came to rescue me and many times God/Universe made it clear I need to rescue myself; no one else can do it. How I started my first realization of this was in my early thirties. I was going through so many of life's changes, constantly feeling I was being hit by wave after wave like I was going to drown in a deep-sea and the more 'waves of life' that hit me the more I felt I was drowning into my dark matter.

I finally went to seek professional help. My therapist was wonderful. I didn't know how valuable each was in my times of need when I was younger. In one case; after a few sessions, my counselor told me: "I want you to go home and write three good things that happen to you each day." "Ok sure, why not," I thought. I didn't know how hard this would be!

A few weeks went by; I was even more depressed then than when I had started therapy! I had not written one thing down. Then one day, I was outside in my backyard thinking, "wow this will never work! Nothing will work; ever work! Why am I even alive?". The infamous question many ask our self at some point in life, during a depressing time. The sun was beaming as I cried and sat on the stoop in the backyard. I had been sitting in my dulled life and having a terrible day (like always, thinking it will never get better!) when suddenly, I saw a ladybug land on the screen of the back door. After some time, I reached over and had him walk on my hand, just enjoying that moment, with the sun keeping me warm. Then he lifted his wings and flew away.

That night, I lay in bed in my 'stinking' thinking mode, trying to think, "what good came of the day?" Suddenly, the ladybug crossed my mind. So, I sat up, turned on the light and wrote: "A Lady Bug!" on a blank piece of paper and then fell fast asleep.

I had a therapy appointment the next morning. I went to it with my piece of paper in hand, still saddened that I did not have three things written down. I gave the piece of paper to my therapist and sat down. She opened it and said, "that's wonderful!" I thought I was going to get chastised, as I had felt leaving the past few appointments; this time for not finding and writing more down. However, after thinking about it, it was me creating that feeling of chastisement inside myself, not her. In addition, looking back, she was the first one in my life at that time who said something positive to me. It had been months not hearing a positive word from someone else. I now realize I said nothing positive to myself, either.

So, I left her office, ran some errands, and went home glum as usual. As I fell asleep, I thought, "oh, what good came out of today?" Immediately, I wrote the good things that happened that day:

1. I wanted to attend my appointment and I showed up. (Accountability).

2. I remembered my paper to show her and to tell her about the ladybug. I felt proud that I had finally actually written something down. (Accountability).

3. I didn't cry when I got home.

4. I ate something I liked, relaxed while I ate. Truthfully not really wanting to eat, but I had brought home a great dish. Afterward, I lay in bed thinking, "wow, today was a great day!" I sang: "You are My Sunshine" to myself before bed.

The next day, I awoke to feel much better. Much more alive than I had felt in a long time. I didn't question it; I just sprang up and started my day as usual. When I had my next therapy appointment, I brought in a small notebook, there were a few pages of things I thought were positive and the things I accomplished. I continued counseling for a few more sessions. I then realized I didn't feel the need to go to therapy every week, so we moved it to every two, then once a month. Eventually, I was stable on my own once again, feeling bright and sunshiny inside and once again outside as well; others noticed.

Now I display my light and positive energy as often as I can, both on the inside as well as the outside. I review my progress when things are looking grim. Now I can glean through the negative, each, and every, time. Many factors can pile up and it does become difficult. So, when I have an obstacle these days, I go right back to my journal, write the good things each day and then look at the progress I have made over each week. Peace and rational thinking begin to kick in gear, solutions show up and I move forward just like everyone else.

I chose to share this story because none of us ever feel great every day and there are times in each of our lives when life just bogs us down, we feel unhappy, discontented feelings and non-fulfillment of life's purpose for oneself.

There are resources out there to be found if you are in need or want to have help. One happens to be my theory: "The Universal Relationship Pyramid," a block-by-block building instruction to finding a healthy relationship with oneself and others.

In my theory, there is a basement of gunk and muck. Here we can become stagnant, stuck, and unhappy. We eventually, after a time, build up resentment and feel as if we are dying or already dead inside. This is a clear sign we need to filtrate the negativity from ourselves. Once we do that, then the positivity can flow back through us. I am a firm believer in this and try to practice the stepping blocks each day in "Geri's World."

By the way, yes, many of us can get to the point of not feeling life is worth it. I was lucky I had some reliable and well-trained people to go to for help. They were able to assist me out of that dark, dingy basement of emotional gunk and muck, into my own light by using their internal light, as I now try and do with others. I am grateful for them and the guiding light that they gave to me in my time of need, as I now use my own light to show others out of their negativity; how to glean their own life and shine brightly for others in their lives. The trickle effect of positivity is a powerful tool to have, to help yourself and another—directly or indirectly—out of the negative into the positive of one's life's journey.

So, my hard work on myself in my younger years (gleaning through all the negative parts of life, truly looking for what was good in each day, holding onto that and moving forward instead of being caught in my own basement of gunk and muck) paid off. Becoming resentful and feeling like I am slowly dying inside is not where I want my heart and soul to live.

That doesn't mean I still don't have those moments. I just no longer allow those moments to be the focus of how I choose to portray my soul to others and myself. I would rather shine as best as I can and as often as I can, to be that ray of sunshine for myself and to be the beacon to others who need a guiding light.

With best regards, deepest feeling, and many blessings, Geri

AUTHOR BIOGRAPHY—Geri Magee, Ph.D.

Geri Magee, PhD, has been working with individuals, couples and families creating a healthy lifestyle for over 32 years.

As a single mother, she worked as a certified Financial and Estate planner for insurance and banking companies establishing and creating new divisions in the finance industry. Later in life she became a Marriage and Family Therapist, Mental Health Counselor for 22 years.

Geri is an Author, Inspirational Writer Motivational Speaker and Mentor. Individual, Couple Counseling and Family Therapy - 22 years. Theorist of the "Universal/Celestial Relationship Pyramid"[vii] for professional or personal use.

Training available. Executive and Therapeutic Mentoring 29 yrs. Financial and Estate Planner.
https://www.facebook.com/Grandma-in-the-Box-
https://www.facebook.com/HRHHC1
https://www.facebook.com/DrGMagee
https://www.facebook.com/DrGeriMagee
Twitter: DrG@DrGMagee
Instagram: DrGMagee

About Karamjeet Kaur

Karamjeet Kaur, MBA, (Ph.D.), Author, Certified Trainer, Self-love Specialist Coach, Certified Mindfulness-Based Stress-Reduction Teacher, Change Consultant, co-founder of Global Homeopathic Centre (GHC) Sdn Bhd and founder of Self-Love Training Academy.

Karamjeet has a background of 20 years working experience in local and multinational (RHB, HSBC, ESPNSTAR SPORTS) organizations. Karamjeet is currently pursuing her Ph.D. (Management) on Self-Love.

Karamjeet is also runner-up winner for the Inspiration Award from Centre of Excellence, UK. She is also an Amazon bestselling author.

Karamjeet has recently been nominated under "Malaysian Successful People" in British Pedia Encyclopedia, Malaysia for 2021 (3rd edition).

Karamjeet has been involved with social work since 2004. She is the one of the founders of Wellness Homeopathy Centre (GHC). GHC provides self-love, homeopathy, MBSR and other holistic treatments. Karamjeet focuses only on self-love empowerment, motivational self-help, and belief-thought patterns. She has been coaching and consulting with patients and clients from all walks of life. She works with her business partner on creating wellness awareness of self-love with patients at GHC.

Karamjeet is conducting free talks to teenagers and women on self-love for NGOs and Secondary Schools. Her first book, "Truly Love Me", was published in 2016 under Balboa Press, Hay House Division, USA.

In 2019, Karamjeet co-authored in the anthology, "Calling All Earth Angels and Healers" compiled by Dr Geri Magee, USA (who is a Quilly® Award winner under Jack Canfield's™ book, "Chicken Soup for the Soul.")

Karamjeet's third book, "Truly Love Within", revised version of Truly Love Me, was published in 2019.

Karamjeet's own anthology, and her fourth book, "Life is a Gift – Loving You", was published in July 2020 with co-authors from around the world. Her aim is all about waking up Self-Love in Humanity.

Karamjeet writes for international online magazines, websites, and co-hosts radio online shows on Empowering True Inner Self with Body Mind Radio, Michigan, USA.

Social Media Platforms:

www.selfloveacademy.com.my

www.lovelifehomeopathy.com

www.facebook.com/selflovetrainingacademy/

www.facebook.com/LoveLifeHomeopathy/

www.instagram.com/karamjeetkaurselflove/

www.linkedin.com/in/karamjeet-kaur-2b7287131/?originalSubdomain=my

End Notes

[i] https://tvbennett.com/
[ii] Aristotle on Self-love. https://escholarship.org/uc/item/30m759kz
https://onlinelibrary.wiley.com/doi/abs/10.1111/j.2041-6962.1989.tb00514.x
[iii] Borenstein, J. (2020, February 12). Self-love and what it means. Self-Love and What It Means | Brain & Behavior Research Foundation.
https://bbrfoundation.org/blog/self-love-and-what-it-means
[iv] https://en.wikipedia.org/wiki/Padre_Pio
https://www.britannica.com/biography/Padre-Pio
[v] https://www.worldpranichealing.com/en/what-is-pranic-healing
[vi] Meditation on twin hearts is one of the most powerful meditation tools for spiritual development. It is a true gift from the great ones". Grand Master Choa Kok Sui. https://pranichealingireland.ie/twin-hearts-meditation/ N.D
[vii] https://www.facebook.com/watch/?v=3549704921753369

Made in the USA
Columbia, SC
25 October 2024